BEGINNING AT JERUSALEM

By
JOSEPH HOFFMAN COHN, D.D.
General Secretary,
American Board of Missions to the Jews, Inc.

Published by
AMERICAN BOARD OF MISSIONS TO THE JEWS, INC.
236 WEST 72ND STREET   NEW YORK 23, N. Y.

Printed in U.S.A.

FOREWORD

by CLARENCE EDWARD MACARTNEY, D.D.

*Minister, First Presbyterian Church,
Pittsburgh, Pa.*

ISRAEL today is passing through a fiery furnace of persecution and trial. Were it not for the mighty assurances of the Word of God concerning the destiny of this people, one might conclude that their annihilation was at hand. These trials and persecutions, and also the survival of Israel, are predicted in the Scriptures. "The Lord shall cause thee to be smitten before thine enemies: thou shalt go out one way against them, and flee seven ways before them: and shalt be removed into all the kingdoms of the earth. . . . And the Lord shall scatter thee among all people, from the one end of the earth even unto the other . . . And among these nations shalt thou find no ease, neither shall the sole of thy foot have rest. . . . And thy life shall hang in doubt before thee . . . In the morning thou shalt say, Would God it were even! and at even thou shalt say, Would God it were morning!" (Deut. 28:25, 64, 65, 66, 67).

These predictions have been fulfilled in the successive waves of invasion which swept over Israel and the captivities which they have endured. In Europe in recent years there have been more terrible persecutions of Israel than at any period in its long history. Yet the nation still survives. This, too, was predicted by the prophets. "Fear thou not, O Jacob my servant, saith the Lord: for I am with thee; for I will make a full end of all the nations whither I have driven thee: but I will not make a full end of thee" (Jer. 46:28).

The Temple of Athena at Athens has been abandoned for ages; but the descendants of Abraham still assemble to worship

God in a synagogue below the Acropolis. I remember walking one day along the banks of the Tiber where I could view the colossal ruins of imperial Rome. That empire and its worship vanished long ago; but there on the banks of the Tiber, where the Caesars once ruled and reigned, and where the Emperor Claudius issued his decree expelling all Jews from the city, I came upon a synagogue where the law of Moses is still read. The nations and kingdoms of the world have passed and disappeared. The Jew remains. His symbol is the burning bush, where God spake to Moses. "The bush burned with fire and the bush was not consumed."

This remarkable survival of Israel in itself would suggest a great future for the Jews. This we find clearly outlined in the Bible. In his famous metaphor of the olive tree St. Paul says that the wild olive branches, that is the Gentiles, have been grafted upon the mother tree. The original branches have been broken off through unbelief. Yet there is hope that they shall be grafted in again. If the unbelief and apostasy of Israel were used of God for the enrichment of the Gentiles, how "much more their fullness?" "If the casting away of them be the reconciling of the world, what shall the receiving of them be but life from the dead?"

I can remember as a child hearing my father quote in his public prayers the words of Zechariah: "In those days it shall come to pass, that ten men shall take hold out of all languages of the nations, even shall take hold of the skirt of him that is a Jew, saying, We will go with you: for we have heard that God is with you" (8:23). Israel has had a great past, and the nation still survives, a mighty witness to the truth of the Scriptures, to the glorious destiny of the Church, and to the future of the human race.

Our Lord's final command to His Church when He was taken up into heaven, was that His disciples were to be witnesses unto Him in Jerusalem, Judea, Samaria, and unto the uttermost part of the earth. The preaching of the Gospel of redemption did, indeed, begin, according to the commandment of Christ, at Jerusalem. But great portions of the Christian Church have forgotten what St. Paul said, how the Gospel is the power of God unto Salvation to everyone that believeth, "to the Jew first." It is not enough that Gentile Christians should be stirred by the great history of Israel, and should believe that great events in the jurisprudence of mankind are linked with the future of Israel. It is our duty to endeavor to give the Gospel to all men, and not neglect to give it to those, who in the providence of God, through our Lord Jesus Christ, first gave it to the world.

In this volume, "Beginning at Jerusalem," Dr. Joseph Hoffman Cohn sets forth earnestly and clearly the claims of Israel upon the Church of Christ. In this day of Israel's anguish and tribulation, let us pray that God will visit and deliver His people, as He has in days gone by. "Pray for the peace of Jerusalem: they shall prosper that love thee."

CONTENTS

Beginning at Jerusalem

ANTHOLOGY ON
TO THE JEW FIRST

Compiled from the files of
THE CHOSEN PEOPLE

RIGHT AND WRONG INTERPRETATIONS
January, 1918

Our Lord Jesus strictly commanded that the preaching of His Gospel should begin at Jerusalem (Luke 24:47; Acts 1:8). The idea latent in the minds of some people that the Gospel was offered to the Jews first by Christ and therefore they had their chance, is not according to the Scriptures. The Jew of today has not had his chance until the Gospel is offered him, not in letter simply, but in a ministry clothed with the power of the Holy Spirit. This command of the Lord was repeated through His servant Paul in the divine order, "To the Jew first" (Romans 1:16). This divine order was carefully observed by Paul, at the hazard of his life, in the ministry of his preaching to the Gentiles, for which he was chosen specially. If we read the Book of Acts with some observation, following him from city to city, we find that in every instance Paul, the special apostle to the Gentiles, entered the synagogue or sought out the Jews and preached "To the Jew first." (Acts 9:20; 14:1; 17:1-16; 19:8; 28:17.) This he did despite repeated rejections, for the Jews of one town cannot be condemned for the neglect of those in another city. How much less can we lay upon the present generation the blame of the rejection by the Jews of two thousand years ago? As long, therefore, as the Gospel is to be preached to every creature, the distinctive order, "to the Jew first and also to the Gentile," must be carried out faithfully in every country and in every generation even until our Lord comes the second time.

The Fatal Blunder

But Christendom has reversed the divine order. Missionaries by thousands have been sent to many different nationalities but not to the Jews. Millions of dollars have been readily spent for educational and philanthropic purposes among the Gentiles. Hospitals, libraries, schools, nurseries, shelters for the friendless, lodging houses, industrial and training schools, and other large and costly institutions have been established in connection with mission work among the Gentiles, but nothing of the kind among the Jews. The American Board of Missions to the Jews had to plead for twenty-two years for a building in which to accommodate the large audiences of Jews that flocked to our doors and also for a training school and some other facilities. An appeal for a shelter for destitute cats and dogs would have brought liberal responses from some of the philanthropists. Those that use their money for such purposes are placing more value upon their own opinion than on that of the Lord Jesus. They believe in Christianity and in the Bible, but only according to their own interpretation.

Christendom has interpreted Jerusalem, Israel and Zion to refer to the Church. "To the Jew first" meant taking the Gospel to the Jew first only in apostolic days, it was, and even now is, asserted. These and many other wrong interpretations of God's Word have set an example to Christian kings and rulers. They have relegated the Lord Jesus and His peace to the celestial regions; they must rule with the sword in their dominion on earth. The principles of the Prince of Peace do not apply to the governments on earth. This is the prevailing opinion, hence there are World Wars.

WHAT *IS* GOD'S PLAN?

January, 1919

May we urge again God's plan for the Jews? If the Bible be true, and if words mean what they say, then it is inevitably true that every real Christian must give the Gospel "to the Jew first." Our Lord's own parting words were, "Beginning at Jerusalem." We resent any perverted interpretation of this phrase as meaning "begin in your home field." It does not mean that, it means just what it says— begin with the Jewish people. We resent further, the absurd avoidance of the issue by the assertion that "the Jews had it first." The mere fact that Jews were given the Gospel nineteen hundred years ago, will never excuse you for neglecting the Jew of today, of this very hour, of this very generation. It is outrageously unfair to judge the Jew of the present day because of what did or did not happen two thousand years ago.

The truth is, that God's plan for world evangelization has never been changed. That plan was, and is now, that we, as believers in the Lord Jesus Christ, shall make known His salvation to all the earth, "To the Jew First." This means that in every generation we are to preach the Gospel to the Jew first. It means, further, that in your church, in your Sunday School, and in your Missionary Society, you are faithfully to follow this divine plan, and you are to set aside unto Him the first part of your offering for missions, to be used in giving the Gospel literally "to the Jew first."

And then the wonderful thing about all this is that the Lord does add His blessing, and He somehow makes the rest of your money accomplish much more in other missionary work than it would have done if you had not given your first offering "to the Jew first." We cannot understand this, nor can we explain it, but we have seen with our own eyes, and we have heard with our own ears, over and over again, that God has blessed in a remarkable way those Christians who have followed this plan. We have in our files innumerable letters from friends, all testifying to the miraculous fact that since they began to give "to the Jew first" the Lord has poured into their lives a new blessing and a new joy. And how could it be otherwise? This people is a peculiar people, a people in a special sense, God's people. How then can you expect that God should not exercise some special care over them? Is it not a natural and a logical thing that if you bless this people, God must bless you?

Be it said, with profound thanksgiving, that year after year the Lord is permitting us to witness an increasing number of Christian people who are awaking to this long-forgotten teaching, and even as we go to press we are receiving scores of letters, all of them telling us in effect, "I am sending you my first offering of the New Year, because I want to give this contribution 'to the Jew first.'"

Dear friend, will you not join such a company? Will you not put God to the test? This principle of giving the Gospel to the Jew first is just as workable and provable in this day of Grace, as was the Mosaic law of the Tithe, "Prove me ... saith the Lord of hosts, if I will not open you the windows of heaven, and pour you out a blessing, that there shall not be room enough to receive it." Malachi 3:10. We urge you to put God to the test. Will you try it?

"BEGIN AT JERUSALEM" — CHRIST DID IT

January, 1920

In accordance with the Scriptures the Lord Jesus took upon Himself a Jewish incarnation, and as a baby, had to be carried in the loving arms of a Jewish mother. "He came to His own." He did not leave them and go to another people. From the beginning of the year unto the end of the year He preached, taught and appealed to the Jews exclusively. When He sent out the Twelve He commanded them saying, "Go not into the way of the Gentiles, and into any city of the Samaritans enter ye not: But go rather to the lost sheep of the house of Israel." Matt. 10:5, 6. Again, His last message on earth was to His followers, that after the Holy Spirit was come upon them, they should be witnesses unto Him both in Jerusalem, and in all Judea, and in Samaria, (mark this divine order) and unto the uttermost part of the earth. Acts 1:8. Then Paul, having the knowledge, by a direct revelation of the Holy Spirit, taught "to the Jew first and also to the Greek," and lived up to this doctrine all his life of missionary zeal and activity. In every generation since, there have been a few, who if not actively engaged in giving the Gospel to the Jews, believed in the Scripture and prayed for that end. By believing in and advocating this teaching of the Scriptures, one sets forth a sure proof of absolute reliance upon God. To such the Holy Spirit addresses those beautiful words of 2 Chron. 16:9, "For the eyes of the Lord run to and fro throughout the whole earth to show Himself strong in the behalf of them whose heart is perfect toward Him." The second part of the same message which reads, "Herein thou hast done foolishly," applies to those who, like King Asa, distrust the Word of God and reverse the divine order.

"PUTTING FIRST THINGS FIRST"

January, 1921

At the beginning of a new year we wish again to knock upon the doors of the hearts of our readers, and to ask an abundant entrance for the message we would bring. It is an old message, but each passing year seems only to give it new emphasis and new brilliancy. It concerns God's fundamental requirement of "putting first things first." And its special application to the missionary program has to do with the need of presenting the Gospel to all peoples, in all ages and generations, in the only order ever sanctioned by God—"to the Jew first." Romans 1:16; Acts 1:8; 13:46.

Kicking Against The Pricks

World War I opened the eyes of many of God's true children to the gross materialism into which organized Christendom had fallen, and they have been amazed and sickened to realize that this organized thing calling itself Christianity has tried to make of itself a world ruler and to dabble in politics and in governments and in economics and in labor—and, in fact, in everything except that to which our Lord called His Church—to be a witness to all the world, a witness concerning Himself, "to the Jew first, and also to the Greek." Of course, it is all easy enough to understand when we carefully analyze it, why such organizations should have no use for God's missionary program—because it conflicts with their own program of world power!

To many earnest Christians the order of "to the Jew first" comes with an unendurable irritation; but we can only explain this strange phenomenon on the ground that such Christians have not yet surrendered their wills wholly to

God's will; and perhaps also there may be left in their hearts just a bit of Gentile antipathy for the Jew, which was not fully taken out at conversion. A friend said to us recently, in all good faith and innocence, "I know when I was fully and thoroughly converted; for it was then that God took all hatred out of my heart, so that now I love everybody—even the Jews!"

We Prefer God's Order To Man's

"But why keep harping on 'to the Jew first'?" a very honored friend asked us some time ago, and then continued, "You don't need that argument in order to get support for your work. You have a hundred better claims to Christian help; the large population, the poverty, the ignorance, the persecution, all these are better arguments." And our answer was, "Because that is God's order, and we prefer His order to any amount of human arguments, however convincing." And not long ago the writer was giving a series of talks in a Christian church, and at the end of the series, one of the leading men in that church said to him, "The most important thing you did for our people has been to show them that God's order is still 'to the Jew first.' As soon as you proved this truth from the Word of God, that settled the whole matter once for all; you did not need to present another single argument—the Word says so, and that is final." And that is our appeal always, to the man to whom a "Thus saith the Lord" means something. It is true, and we would be the first one to grant it, that sometimes we cannot understand why God says it, but the mere fact that God does say it, gives us all the why we want. For God's ways are not our ways, and His thoughts are not our thoughts.

The Far-reaching Justice Of God

And yet, it has always seemed to us that there is a broad principle of justice underlying this inscrutable order, "to the Jew first." Not that we would try to justify God in His methods, for if you should ask us off-hand why God established this remarkable order in missions, we should spontaneously reply, "because He is God, and He willed it so." And there you have God's sovereignty, which is as unexplainable as is the Trinity, or Election, or Predestination, or any other of God's wonders.

But we are human, and given to speculative thinking. And we often try to get a philosophical explanation of God's spiritual laws; and sometimes such an explanation is helpful, provided it is subjected to God's standards. And it is in this light that we often think of the justice of God's order in Missions—"to the Jew first." And we study history, and we find a few great outstanding facts in relation to the Jews which throw much light on this interesting subject.

In the first place, the Jews have suffered much. They have been drowned; they have been burned at the stake; they have been massacred by the sword and gun; they have undergone tortures unparalleled in the history of any other nation. But the suffering itself, however intense, would hardly establish a sound claim upon us for Gospel effort, for we might answer that other people have also suffered—the Armenians, for instance. The thing that settles the claim, however, is the horrible fact that all of the Jewish suffering has always come through people who called themselves Christians, so that to the Jewish mind Christianity has become synonymous with blood-thirstiness and anti-semitism. Who shall say, then, that we ought not to present the Gospel in its true light "to the Jew first", so as to remove from Christianity the black stain of the centuries? Is it not only a matter of justice that these Jews, who have only known of Christianity through wild and savage orgies of bloodshed, shall now know of it through the gentle ministrations of Christ's true followers? Isaiah 40:1-2 throws much light on this point, "Comfort ye, comfort ye my people, saith your God. Speak ye comfortably to Jerusalem, and cry unto her, that her warfare is accomplished, that her iniquity is pardoned: for she hath received of the Lord's hand double for all her sins." And if God has declared that they have suffered enough for their sins, surely none of us would dare say, "let them suffer—it's coming to them."

And then, secondly, through these Jews God chose to give to the world His oracles, as is declared in Romans 3:1. God might have given His Word through the Egyptians, or the Babylonians; but He didn't, He gave it through the Jews. And this gives the Jews an advantage "much every way." And not the least of this advantage must be their right to receive in these days of their darkness and exile the message of comfort, of individual salvation through the Lord Jesus Christ.

God Loves The Jews

Thirdly, God loves them. This great fact almost shrieks its importance at us from every page of the Word of God, so that it hardly needs even the stating. Such a passage as Isaiah 49:15 is typical of God's attitude to Israel—"Can a woman forget her sucking child, that she should not have compassion on the son of her womb? yea, they may forget, yet will I not forget thee. Behold, I have graven thee upon the palms of my hands; thy walls are continually before me." Surely no true child of God can afford to hate what God loves; and here we have another valid claim established for giving the Gospel "to the Jew first."

Then fourthly, we ought never to forget that those first missionaries that braved the storms and the jails and the tortures of a Gentile world in order to give those Gentiles the knowledge of Christ, were all Jews. If Paul, the Hebrew, had not said "I am debtor to the Greeks and to the barbarians," perhaps many Gentiles who now rejoice in salvation might have been savages and aliens from God. Surely, a sense of common gratitude for blessings received would cause us gladly to concede to the Jew a place of honor in our Gospel program "to the Jew first."

And then, fifthly, and finally, many of His true children are earnestly looking for the early return of our Lord, and they are putting forth every effort to hasten His coming. To all such we would say that there is no surer way of hastening this blessed fulfillment of His promise than by evangelizing the Jews. The reasons for this are many, but two are of special interest here:

First, we know that our Lord will come for His Church, His Body, as soon as that Body is complete, that is, as soon as the full number has been added to the Church. We also know that the true Church must be composed of both Jews and Gentiles, otherwise we make a farce out of such a passage as Ephesians 2:14, "For He is our peace, who hath made both one, and hath broken down the middle wall of partition between us." If these statements are true, then it logically follows that since historically there have been so few Jews in the Church of Christ, and since by a corrupting process of decay the domination of Christianity has gradually passed into the control of Gentile hands, the proportion of Jews in the Church today is so small as to be infinitesimal. And when we realize this sad fact, then it must come to us almost as a revelation, that surely there must be many more Jews saved before we can consider His Church as truly complete. Otherwise, the middle wall of partition has never been broken down.

Secondly, it was only to Jews that our Lord said in Matthew 23:29, "For I say unto you, Ye shall not see me henceforth, till ye shall say, Blessed is he that cometh in the name of the Lord." Which, if we interpret Scripture aright, means to us that whenever the Jews as a nation accept Him as Lord and Saviour, then He will come. And who does not long for His appearing? And who does not realize that unless He does soon appear, this world is doomed to a horrible cataclysm the like of which has not been duplicated in history?

These are some of the reasons which seem to us to place the program of missions—"to the Jew first"—on a basis of divine justice. And we present them to you for the strengthening of your convictions in these matters, and for the deepening of the loyalty you have so generously shown to this Mission established on that fundamental principle of Scripture. So that together we may continue to labor, and to spend and be spent, until that Day shall dawn when time shall be no more, and we, reigning with Him, shall behold the result of our having obeyed Him while we were here on this earth; and we shall all rejoice and be glad in Him.

TO THE JEW—LAST? OR NOT AT ALL?

January, 1922

To the Jew—Last! We are going to reverse the order! For sometimes it is a good thing to take a look in the glass and "see ourselves as others see us." For a number of years, in January, we have been in the habit of writing an expository article on the foundation missionary principle, "To the Jew First," as taught in the Scriptures. Many hundreds of our readers, with minds unprejudiced, and eager to be taught of the Holy Spirit, have come to see this vital truth, and one of the gratifying experiences that we have each year is to receive, in January, scores of letters which say in substance, "I want to begin the year by making my first missionary gift, to the Jew first." Even as we write these lines, a letter comes to us from a pastor's wife in Canada, a little bit ahead of time, to be sure, but showing the fine motive and heart's desire, and none the less welcome:—"Am enclosing our 'To the Jew first' missionary Christmas remembrance. At the last missionary meeting of our church missionary society, I gave an address on the subject 'To the Jew First,' and hope to do so at least twice a year as long as I am affiliated with any missionary society. To our people here this subject and the truth of it is entirely new, but we are beginning to see that it is taking root in the minds and hearts of a few."

Brickbats With The Bouquets

But a season is not made up only of sunshine, and often in the same mail, letters will travel together, one containing the greatest cheer and encouragement in the work; the other condemning and abusing us for what the writer calls our bigoted and long-discarded theory of "To the Jew First."

And it is strange how indignant and abusive some Christians can become when they disagree with us on this question.

But let us, for a little while, take these "Jew last" exponents on their own ground, and let us examine pragmatically just where their position would lead them. Because, after all, the best way to test out a theory is by the pragmatic test —how does it actually work out in practice?

And, hard as it is to say it, and hard as it will be for many to believe it, the truth is, that usually the person who resents the Scriptural method of missionary work, "To the Jew first," really believes in a doctrine all of his own, which, briefly stated, is "To the Jew not at all!" And the proof of this conclusion can be very easily obtained by your making inquiry from any Christian layman, or pastor, or church, or society which believes that the Jew should not be first, but should "be treated like any other race," and ask such people, "How much did you do for the Jews last year?" We assure you that the silence will be so profound that you can almost hear it.

Revealing A Shameful Motive

To illustrate what we mean, we will quote from two letters received within a few days of each other, and we will let them speak for themselves. The first one is from a warm friend, a pastor, who loves Israel, and who gives us a revelation of conditions in the church he formerly served. For obvious reasons we will omit names and locations:

"Personally my family and myself had come into touch with your work while we were serving ... church in C ... Ohio, when Joseph Cohn visited us. Having had my interest deeply quickened on that occasion and kept at white heat by the monthly visits of your paper, it did not take me long to open my church here at E. to Rev. Mr. Solin. In the C ...

Church, I was rather severely criticised for admitting Joseph Cohn, because some of the officers begrudged the few dollars he received, of which they had personally given nothing. But an interest was kindled there, which has continued despite all. I doubt whether Joseph could get in there again, because the present pastor is not interested. Undoubtedly, many of the people would be glad to see and hear him again. Thus, shortsighted leaders hinder the Lord's cause."

Just think of the "evil eye" attitude of these leaders who had themselves given nothing, but who resented bitterly any one else's giving a dollar! And think of what that poor pastor had to suffer because he opened his heart to Israel's need! And this is the twentieth century of Christianity!

But here is another letter. It, too, speaks for itself, only this time from a layman's standpoint:

"A month or two ago, I received a letter from your mission asking if we would like a meeting at our church by one of your workers. Personally, I favored it and brought it to the attention of our pastor, Rev.... of the Congregational Church of ... but he did not favor it for the reason that our church and benevolent expenses are unusually heavy this year, and that it would not be the best thing to take up an additional collection for the Jewish work. I did not argue the point with him, though I did not agree with him. I do not think we would hurt ourselves in any way to open our church at least once a year to this work; in fact, I believe we ought to do it and that it would be a benefit to us, as well as to the Jewish cause itself. Whatever I can do, within reason, to help your work along, I am willing to do; and I await your pleasure. It will be one of the grandest things that can happen to the world to have the Jewish people brought to Christ, whom they have rejected so long, and to their own detriment."

Now, friend, which would you rather be? A believer in "To the Jew first" doctrine, or a believer in "To the Jew not at all" policy? Do you wonder that these great denominations are now proclaiming their financial distresses all over the land? Is it a wonder that practically all the Boards are deep in the morass of deficits and debts and ruin-staring wreckage? How can God bless such disobedience to His well-defined and established laws?

As for us, we are giving ourselves no worry or anxiety; this is the Lord's work, and He cares for it wondrously well. While all around us they are crying "deficits," "retrenchment," "bankruptcy," the Lord has given this Mission the largest income of its history, and He has enabled us to take forward steps in Jewish evangelism that will prove most effective in their results. The Lord is our banker, He takes care of our needs; and year by year the host increases who write us, "I want to start this year right. Here is my gift, 'To the Jew first.'"

Will you be one of this host for this new year?

BY THEIR FRUITS

January, 1923

When John sent two of his disciples to ask Jesus, "Art thou he that should come?" he received a remarkable answer: "Go and shew John again those things which ye do hear and see: The blind receive their sight and the lame walk, the lepers are cleansed, and the deaf hear, the dead are raised up, and the poor have the gospel preached to them." In other words, if a man doubts the efficiency of an electric battery, don't argue with him; just ask him to put his hands on the wires, and then, *turn on the current!*

And this is apropos of the fact that it has been, to us, a rather pleasant custom to write a homily in these columns every first month of the year, on the text, "To the Jew First." Whether the reading of these expositions has been as pleasant to all of our readers as the writing of them has been to us, we are not so sure; indeed, if our files could talk they could tell of many an angry letter that was laid peacefully to rest in their silent caverns, letters that railed at us because we insisted on such an old and such a literal interpretation of this divinely ordained method for world missions. And it always has been hard for us to understand why a Christian should be so angry when we held so closely to the Word of God, and why it should hurt such a Christian to have us proclaim this doctrine in our columns. Surely, we have done him no harm, while, on the contrary, many thousands of God's children have borne testimony to marvelous blessings experienced by them as a direct result of their obeying literally in their own Christian lives, God's missionary method for this age, "To the Jew First." Take, for instance, as only one illustration, the case of the Wealthy Street Baptist Church of Grand

Rapids, which, together with its faithful pastor, Dr. Van Osdel, has stood as a granite wall in its friendship and support of this Mission for the past ten or twelve years. In a recent issue of their weekly paper, *The Baptist Temple News*, they give a report of the Annual Conference on Prophecy and the Jews held in their church last October; in that report there appears an illuminating paragraph which we think it would be worth while for every true Christian church to read and ponder over:

The Wealthy Street Baptist Church has for some time been the largest single contributor to this work. We believe the phenomenal growth of the Wealthy Street Baptist Church in the past few years, is a direct result of obeying the Scriptural injunction in their missionary giving and in their plans "To the Jew First."

But we are not going to argue this matter this time. Instead, we are going to use the method of the Lord Jesus Christ in the Scripture passage above quoted, and in a sort of paraphrase of our Lord's words, we would now say to all objectors, opposers and questioners, as regards the doctrine of "To the Jew First," "Go and see for yourself that wherever this divine injunction has been faithfully followed, there you will find that God has added His blessing in such an outpouring of His Spirit that the results sent their echo around the world." In other words, *it works!* And it works both ways; it blesses those who obey this law and it blesses the seed sown so that a Jewish conversion literally fulfills the promise of Romans 11: 15, of "life from the dead."

Horatius Bonar Speaks

Take the marvelous growth of the great Free Church of Scotland; how many people know that when those 473 weak and hated little churches pulled out and met together in the first great convention to establish the Free Church of Scotland, that great saint, Horatius Bonar, rose before those delegates and made an impassioned plea that God could not bless the new united Free Churches of Scotland unless they then and there established as a part of their doctrinal program the divine order in Missions as being "To the Jew First." And sure enough, those delegates unanimously accepted that challenge and appointed Dr. Bonar himself with Robert Murray McCheyne as a committee to go immediately on a missionary tour throughout the European continent and into the Holy Land, and to establish Jewish mission stations wherever it was found possible to do so; and during the absence of these saints of God, God sent a mighty revival which began in Dr. McCheyne's Church and spread throughout all of the Free Churches of Scotland; not only this, but the result of the establishing of these Jewish mission stations throughout Europe at that time was that some of the greatest preachers and theologians among the Jewish Christians of the last century were the direct product of those missions. Who shall venture an estimate of the value in dollars and cents of these Jewish Christian scholars to the Christian world?

A Galaxy Of Shining Stars

And then to go a bit farther; take the case of the London Jewish Missionary Society, which likewise established itself on the bed-rock principle of giving the Gospel to the Jew first. Who shall measure the value to the world of men like Bishop Schereschewsky, Dr. Edersheim, Adolph Saphir, and the numerous host of other equally brilliant Jews who were led to the knowledge of the Lord Jesus Christ through this particular missionary agency? How many millions of dollars will you put as the value of Bishop Schereschewsky's translation of the English Bible into the Mandarin tongue, a translation which enabled the Christian Church to reach in one sweep a population of Chinese numbering 250,000,000?

And consider the respect, often amounting to veneration, which wide circles of Christians—and not Christians only— had for men like Bishop Alexander, Bishop Hellmuth, Bishop Schereschewsky; for men like Professor Neander, "the last Church Father," whose lecture room in Berlin was for years crowded with enthusiastic students from every country in Europe; or Professor Caspary, of Christiania, who has been called, "The teacher of Scandinavia"; or Professor Cassel, of whom the *Jewish Chronicle* of January 1st, 1880, said that "A genius like Cassel is always an honour to his former brethren in faith." If the representatives of the German people thought the Jewish Christian, Martin E. Simson, worthy to preside over the great National Congress of 1848; if Queen Victoria honoured with her friendship Christian Jews like Disraeli and Felix Mendelssohn; if, on the authority of Lord Acton, we are led to believe that the converted Jew, Frederick Stahl, "had a more predominant influence on public affairs, and showed more political ability than even Lord Beaconsfield"; do you not see how important a place these Jewish Christians filled in the world's Christian progress?

And then consider further what high qualities of heart and mind must have gone to the making of men like David Ginsburg and Moses Margoliouth, Alfred Edersheim and Adolph Saphir. Everyone of them came as a stranger and foreigner, without any friends or connections, to England, and everyone of them lived to be honored by the friendship of some of the best and most highly placed men of that country, men like Lord Shaftesbury, Mr. Gladstone, Sir Edward Clarke, and others. Ginsburg and Margoliouth were both on the Revision Committee of the Old Testament, while

Edersheim and Saphir have enriched the theological literature of England with works of abiding value.

A perusal of one of the clerical directories of the Church of England will show how many Mocattas, Montefiores, Pereiras, da Silvas, Ricardos, not to speak of the many Cohens, Levis, Isaacs, Jacobs, etc., there are among the English clergy—all of them English Jews, or the sons of English Jews whose families ranked with the best, the most aristocratic, of them all.

Higher Yet The Stars Ascend

And the same can be said of Holland, Denmark and Sweden, for we meet among the converts there the honored names of Dr. Abraham Capadose, Isaac Da Costa, one of Holland's best poets, Sir Moses Salvador, van Ronkel, the Belmontes, Professor Josephson of Upsala, Professor David of Copenhagen, the Danish poet Henrik Herz, Dr. Kalkar, and many more.

Do you not see that whenever and wherever the true Christian will lay his hand upon the Jew to do him good in accordance with the plan of God, somehow blessing must come out of it? There is a sort of unexplainable element about it all that can only be attributed to the supernatural. And if this is so, may we not ask you to think over these things again at this time of the year, because this is the time when we do think over in retrospect as well as in prospect those deeper things which tend to shape our lives for good or for ill.

The majority of our readers have been for years thoroughly convinced in their own minds and hearts that this program of "To the Jew First" actually works, and each January, we suppose largely as a matter of sentiment, we receive an increasing number of gifts accompanied by letters which say in their general tenor, "I want to make this, my first gift of the new year, to the Jew first."

But we are addressing these lines now particularly to those of our friends who have not yet come up with us on these higher levels and we would ask of you, will you not join these ranks, and try for one year to follow out literally and consistently this divinely ordained plan, "To the Jew first"?

IT MIGHT HAVE BEEN

January, 1924

God's laws cannot be broken with impunity. This is true whether the transgressor be a child of God or a child of the devil. The only difference is that a child of God receives his punishment a bit more swiftly and perhaps more directly than the out and out sinner, for we know that "whom the Lord loveth, He chasteneth." That is to say, God cares enough about His own child to give him quick correction. So we have many illustrations in the Word of just how God has acted under varied circumstances; with a Pharaoh, for instance, He sends a Moses and an Aaron, not once, but many times; and plagues, not once, but ten times; and finally He sends destruction. But to a David he sends Nathan swiftly, and a speedy punishment. With a Sodom, long patience, then brimstone and fire; with a Moses quick chastisement for disobedience. In other words, the more precious we are to Him, the more prompt the discipline.

This is an interesting study, in view of the recent outburst of apostasy which America has witnessed in the bold and blatant denial of those things in the Word of God which are most surely known among us who are His truly born-again children. The Virgin birth of our Lord, His literal resurrection, the infallibility of His Word, these verities of our faith have been given the lie by men who call themselves ministers of the Gospel. Baptists, Methodists, Episcopalians, Presbyterians—all, all, are bitten with the same poison. Dr. Munhall, in *The Eastern Methodist* of November 15th, says virtually, "I cannot name one Methodist minister on Manhattan Island who believes the whole counsel of God and who holds forth the Word of life!" And Dr. A. T. Pierson used to say, "I don't know of a church in all Brooklyn where I could go and hear the Word of God expounded and believed."

Now a logical person knows that for every effect there is somewhere a cause. And we would do well to hunt assiduously for the cause, or causes, that have brought about a situation where God and His Word are being blasphemed shamelessly week after week in some of the leading pulpits of our land.

Getting Down To The Roots

Some nineteen hundred years ago, God, through His last revelation, the New Testament, gave us a command—in fact, it was our Lord's *last* command before His departure into the clouds. That command was to preach the Gospel to all nations, but *beginning at Jerusalem*. (Luke 24:46, 47). Note this carefully because it contains a distinct and specific direction as to the order of procedure—beginning at Jerusalem; and as later amplified in the Acts and the Epistles, the command found expression in the trenchant phrase, "To the Jew First." (Romans 1:16). This doctrine was well understood by the early Christians, for over and over again we are told that the apostles went, as was their custom, "to the Jew first!" Acts 17:1-4.

A Million Jews—Believers!

And what happened? God blessed marvelously their testimony, and thousands were saved. The 3,000 converts on the day of Pentecost were all Jews. The 5,000 mentioned in Acts 4:4, were all Jews. Neander, the church historian, estimates that there were fully a million Jews who accepted the Lord Jesus Christ as Saviour, in the first century of the Christian era.

But there came a sad day in the history of the Christian

church. Just as in Egypt "there arose a new king who knew not Joseph," so in the early days of the Church there arose a Gentile supremacy which forbode evil for the Jews. The old and valiant Jewish missionaries had died; Paul was gone, Peter was gone; no more were their voices heard in thundering and authoritative instruction "to the Jew first." In their stead arose new leaders who "knew not Joseph." And the Church became then and there paganized, for with the "conversion" of Constantine, the seeds of all the present-day corruption and apostasy were sown.

And that was the Church which began, instead of giving the Gospel to the Jew first, to give hatred, and massacre, and deliberately planned bloodshed, to the Jew first! And those Jews, who might have continued, as they did in the first century, to give to the whole world their unimpeachable testimony to the authority of God's Word, to the necessity for the blood atonement, to the essential imperative of the Virgin birth, those Jews were cast out and cursed.

The Fountain Turns Bitter

And then, after centuries of patience on God's part, He allowed a Jew, Spinoza, to become the father of modern Higher Criticism! The very fountain which God intended to be for the refreshing of all the Gentile world, the Gentiles themselves turned into a poison well, from which all the murky streams of doubt and denial and blasphemy have had their source to this day. And even at the present hour, these poor deluded Gentile ministers think they are giving out something original when they deny the Word of God, while as a matter of fact they are feeding on the husks which the Spinoza school of philosophers threw in the trough for them many years ago, and the Jewish "scholars" of the present day, many of them in high places of learning, in universities, in laboratories, in observatories, all rejoice, because they say, "these Christians are fast becoming Jews."

A Bulwark Against Paganism

Can anything be plainer than this? Do you not see what an awful mistake, not to say sin, has been committed when the Church failed to place the Gospel upon the only sound, scriptural basis, "to the Jew first"? And could anything be more logical than that we should go "to the Jew first"? Think you that if the churches today were filled with Jewish Christians, they would tolerate a preacher who "had his doubts" about the blessed and holy person of the Lord Jesus Christ? Don't you see, if it be true that our Lord came to break down the middle wall of partition between Jew and Gentile and make them one in the body of Christ, then in order to have a true New Testament Church, we must have both Jew and Gentile in that Church? And when, on the contrary, we have today a Church made up practically alto- gether of Gentiles, may we not find here a cause for the paganistic trend in the Church? And so we have in one church here in New York, bare-footed girls dancing on the platform to the sensuous melodies of pagan music—with colored lights to give "inspiration" to the soul! And all this in a Christian Church at a regular Sunday service.

Do you see why we stress so much, "to the Jew first"? It's not done lightly, we assure you; and it is not pleasant to be hated as we sometimes are, because we insist on God's order in Missions. But we long ago were profoundly con- vinced that no other way exists for true blessing and pros- perity to come to the Church unless she repented of her sin and turned again with apostolic fervor, "to the Jew first." And we cast the die, and there we have stood all these years. And gradually, but surely and solidly, a child of God here and one there began to see the light, and we have been joined by a host of true believers who say with us, "The Gospel must be administered in God's order." And many of us have experienced how wonderfully God has blessed us in this new obedience.

Jewish Missions Are Double-barrelled

You can't lose in Jewish missions. Your testimony now will not only complete the body of Christ, and thus bring quickly that day when He "shall descend from heaven with a shout"; but it will also sow the seed and fertilize the soil so that in the terrible day of Jacob's trouble, which shall culminate in Israel's national salvation at the Mount of Olives, the Jews who will be in Jerusalem then, from all parts of the world, will say, "We remember now the words of those missionaries who told us to believe in the Lord Jesus Christ." And because we have been faithful now, they will have salvation then!

Every January brings to us an increasing number of gifts, "To the Jew first." And many letters tell us, "Thank you so much for calling my attention to my duty and privilege. I want to start the New Year right."

Think it over. For some day you too will join this blessed host and you too will say, "I want to preach God's Gospel in God's way—to the Jew first." And while you think it over, just bear in mind that there are today nearly 2,000,000 Jewish souls in New York City who have never even been given the Gospel "to the Jew last"!

IT WAS NECESSARY

January, 1925

"To the Jew first" finds its greatest opposition among those Christians who are least informed concerning the Word of God. And conversely, this vital missionary doctrine finds support among the profoundest of Bible students—men and women who have spent years of deep searching into the sacred truths of God's revelation.

A letter comes to us from a dear friend, in which occurs this sentence: "After a long study of the Book of Romans, I am convinced the Gospel must be given to the Jew first." And sometime ago, in California, a consecrated child of God said to us, "The Book of Ephesians opened my eyes to see that God's unchangeable order for the Gospel in this age is to the Jew first." And still another friend told us once, "The more I study the Acts of the Apostles, the more clearly do I see how fundamentally correct is your missionary doctrine, to the Jew first."

In other words, no matter where the sincere child of God takes up His Word, he will find the same inviolate counsel declared, with nowhere a contradictory phrase.

It is a categorical imperative; it allows no room for argument or philosophizing. It is a thing that must of necessity be done, whether we like it or not. Acts 13:46 throws a searchlight on what we are trying to say:—"It was *necessary* that the word of God should first have been spoken to you." Paul had no choice in the matter—it was necessary! And that *necessity* has never been cancelled by God from that day to this! True, the Church has often cancelled it, but this can only be said to her shame, for whenever that has been done it was only done in direct disobedience to the revealed will of God.

The sainted Scotch preacher, Robert Murray McCheyne, became, early in his ministry, profoundly convinced of the importance of the "To the Jew first" doctrine, and this conviction influenced his life activities. We came across, recently, a sermon of his dealing with this very subject, and we can do our readers no greater service than to give at least some important extracts:

"Paul glories in the Gospel as the power of God unto salvation to the Jew first; from which I draw this Doctrine— that the Gospel should be preached first to the Jews.

"(1) Because judgment will begin with them—'Indignation and wrath to the Jew first,' Romans 2:6-10. It is an awful thought that the Jew will be the first to stand forward at the bar of God to be judged. When the great white throne is set, and He sits down upon it, from Whose face the heavens and earth flee away, and great and small stand before God, is it not a striking thought that Israel—poor, blinded Israel—will be the first to stand in judgment before God?

"Is this not reason, then, why the Gospel should first be preached to the Jew? They are ready to perish. The cloud of indignation and wrath that is even now gathering above the lost will break first upon the head of unhappy, unbelieving Israel. And have you none of the bowels of Christ in you, that you will not run first to them that are in so sad a case?

A Desperate Case

"In a hospital the kind physician runs first to that bed where the sick man lies who is nearest to die. When a ship is sinking, and the gallant sailors have left the shore to save the sinking crew, do they not stretch out the arm of help first to those that are readiest to perish beneath the waves? And shall we not do the same for Israel? The billows of God's anger are ready to dash first over them—shall we not seek to bring them first to the Rock that is higher than they? Their case is more desperate than that of other men—shall we not bring the Good Physician to them, Who alone can bring health and cure? For the Gospel is the power of God unto salvation, to the Jew first, and also to the Greek.

"(2) It is like God to care first for the Jews. It is the chief glory and joy of a soul to be like God. Too many rest in the joy of being forgiven, but our truest joy is to be like Him. We should be like Him in understanding, in will, in holiness, and also in His peculiar affections. 'Love is of God; and every one that loveth is born of God, and knoweth God. He that loveth not knoweth not God; for God is love.' But the whole Bible shows that God has a peculiar affection for Israel. You remember, when the Jews were in Egypt sorely oppressed by their taskmasters, God heard their cry, and appeared to Moses; 'I have seen. I have seen the affliction of my people . . . and I have heard their cry, for I know their sorrows.' And, again, when God brought them through the wilderness, Moses tells them why He did it: 'The Lord did not set his love upon you, nor choose you, because ye were more in number than any people; for ye were the fewest of all people: but because the Lord loved you.' Deut. 7:7, 8. Strange, sovereign, most peculiar love! He loved them because He loved them. Should we not be like God in this peculiar attachment?

"But you say, God has sent them into captivity. Now, it is true God has scattered them into every land, 'The precious sons of Zion, comparable to fine gold, how are they esteemed as earthen pitchers!' Lam. 4-2. But what says God of this? 'I have forsaken mine house, I have left mine heritage; I have given the dearly beloved of my soul into the hand of her enemies.' Jer. 12:7. It is true that Israel is given for a little moment into the hands of her enemies, but it is as true that they are still the dearly beloved of His soul. Should we not give them the same place in our heart which God gives them in His heart? Shall we be ashamed to cherish the same affection which our Heavenly Father cherishes? Shall we be ashamed to be unlike the world and like God in this peculiar love for captive Israel?

Has God Cast Off The Jews?

"But, you say, God has cast them off. 'God hath not cast away his people which he foreknew.' God forbid! The whole Bible contradicts such an idea. 'Zion said, The Lord hath forsaken me, and my Lord hath forgotten me. Can a woman forget her sucking child, that she should not have compassion on the son of her womb? Yea, they may forget, yet will I not forget thee.' Isa. 49:15. 'And so all Israel shall be saved; as it is written. There shall come out of Sion the Deliverer, and shall turn away ungodliness from Jacob.' Now, the simple question for each of you is, Should we not share with God in His peculiar affection for Israel? If we are filled with the Spirit of God, should we not love as He loves? Should we not grave Israel upon the palms of our hands and resolve that through our mercy they also may obtain mercy?

"(3) Because they will give life to the dead world. I have often thought that a reflective traveler, passing through the countries of the world, and observing the race of Israel in every land, might be led to guess, merely from the light of his natural reason, that that singular people are preserved for some great purpose in the world. There is a singular fitness in the Jew to be the missionary of the world. They have not that peculiar attachment to home and country which we have. They are in some measure acquainted with all the languages of the world. But what says the Word of God? 'It shall come to pass, that as ye were a curse among the heathen, O house of Judah, and house of Israel, so will I save you, and ye shall be a blessing.' (Zech. 8:13). To this day they are a curse among all nations, by their unbelief, by their coveteousness; but the time is coming when they shall be as great a blessing as they have been a curse. 'And the remnant of Jacob shall be in the midst of many people as a dew from the Lord, as the showers upon the grass, that tarrieth not for man, nor waiteth for the sons of men.' Micah 5:7. Just as we have found among the parched hills of Judah that the evening dew, coming silently down, gave life to every plant, making the grass to spring, and the flowers to put forth their sweetest fragrance, so shall converted Israel be when they come as dew upon a dead, dry world. 'In those days it shall come to pass that ten men shall take hold, out of all languages of the nations, even shall take hold of the skirt of him that is a Jew, saying, We will go with you; for we have heard that God is with you.' Zech. 8:23. This never has been fulfilled; but, as the Word of God is true, this is true.

" 'Go and preach the Gospel to all nations' said the Saviour. Let us obey His word like little children. All that we plead for is that in sending out missionaries to the heathen, we may not forget to begin at Jerusalem. If Paul be sent to the Gentiles, let Peter be sent to the twelve tribes that are scattered abroad; and let not a by-corner in your hearts be given to this cause, let it not be an appendix to the other doings of the Church, but rather let there be written on the forefront of your hearts, 'To the Jew first' and 'Beginning at Jerusalem.'

Pray For The Jews

"Lastly, because there is a great reward. 'Blessed is he that blesseth thee; cursed is he that curseth thee.' 'Pray for the peace of Jerusalem; they shall prosper that love thee.' We have felt this in our own souls. Your souls shall be enriched also if this cause finds its right place in your affections. We must not only be evangelistic, but evangelistic as God would have us to be—not only dispense the light on every hand, but dispense it first to the Jew. Then shall God revive His work in the midst of the years, and your own souls become like a well-watered garden."

Again we extend the invitation: Will you not try God for this year by writing "to the Jew first" in your missionary program; and then wait and see what blessings the Lord will pour into your life? Year after year each January, we have given this invitation to our readers, and year after year the response has been increasingly large; and year after year have come letters like this: "Thank you for the light on the Jew first: I want to begin the new year with a gift to the Jew first."

How about you? Won't you try it?

HAVE YOU BEEN OBEDIENT?

January, 1926

For some years past it has been our custom in January to say a few words concerning God's divinely ordained missionary plan for this age, "To the Jew First." Recently, our friend and sister in the Lord, Mrs. Jessie Sage Robertson, of Piedmont, Calif., wrote a very helpful article on the same subject, in her little publication, "My Watch." We asked her permission to reprint the article in THE CHOSEN PEOPLE and she has graciously given us her consent. So here it is and may every reader of THE CHOSEN PEOPLE find in it real blessing and a new illumination concerning God's plan for these days:

Can you say with Paul, in Romans 1: 16, "For I am not ashamed of the Gospel of Christ: for it is the power of God unto salvation to every one that believeth; *To the Jew First*"?

This is God's order, have you been obedient? It does indeed "seem easier to see the need of the Chinese or African, thousands of miles away, than of the Jew in our own country." O, beloved, why do you suppose God has brought the Jew, above all others, to our very doors? Is it not that we should have no excuse before Him, for our fulfillment of His order in Romans 1: 16? If the Church had only been obedient here, many a Saul of Tarsus might long since have become a mighty giant among our Christian teachers, such as was Paul. The world might have been evangelized long ago if we had but done exactly what God has told us to do— O, how the work languishes for lack of Pauls and Peters.

There is a very marked undercurrent of Jew hate abroad in the world today. Fully equipped with the Word of God, no real Christian will be drawn into its undertow. The pity of it is, however, that so few are so equipped, for many seem to know only so much of it as others quote to them, and are at the mercy of those who "wrest the Scriptures" on the Jew question.

It will not do to divorce John 1:11 from John 1:12. It will not do to harp on Luke 23:21 and forget all about Luke 23:34. It will not do to split Acts 2:23 and make a case out against the Jews with its last clause, for the first clause states plainly that it was by "the determinate counsel and foreknowledge of God" that the Lord Jesus was "slain" by them. If you divorce the crucifixion of the Lord Jesus at the hands of the Jews from the absolute necessity of it, down to its smallest detail, you might just as well close your Bibles so far as the "rightly dividing word of truth" pertaining to this matter is concerned. It will not do to concentrate only on those who cried, "Away with Him! Crucify Him!" and forget that believing "multitude" of Jews who staged for us our first "Palm Sunday" upon that historic entrance of the Lord Jesus into Jerusalem, Nisan 10th, just four days prior to His crucifixion on Nisan 14th, crying: "Blessed be the king that cometh in the name of the Lord: Peace in heaven, and glory in the highest." (Luke 19:37, 38). Nor will it do for us to forget for one moment, that all we have and are in the way of Christian civilization we owe to these same Jews. "Wherefore remember ... (that) now in Christ Jesus ye who sometimes were far off are made nigh by the blood of Christ." Ephesians 2:12.

Breaking Down The Middle Wall

O beloved, we cannot go to the Jews with a New Testament in our hands and point them to "the Lamb of God which taketh away the sin of the world," which was slain by them in the eternal counsels of the Godhead for themselves and us, if deep down in our hearts there is any Jew hatred. No Jew-hating heart can hope to preach Christ with any acceptance to the Jew—and yet it is the Church's first business to carry her message of the Cross "to the Jew First." The very first business of the Cross, after the blood shed there has been applied to our own hearts, is to break down "the middle wall of partition" between Jew and Gentile. (Ephesians 2: 14). Is that what it has done for you, my brother? my sister? Or has the Cross brought greater enmity into your heart for the Jew?

Do search your heart as you kneel at the foot of that Cross where your Lord and Saviour died for you, and hear Him say with His dying breath, "Forgive them." All enmity melts there, and there it is that "the middle wall of partition" will break down. No more Jew-hating when Jesus the Jew looks down from the Cross into our hearts, and we hear Him cry out from the depths of His breaking heart: "Forgive them."

Now, dear reader, after you have read the above, may we once more extend the invitation: Will you not try God for this year, by writing, "To the Jew First," into your missionary program; and then wait and see what blessings the Lord will pour into your life? Year after year, each January we have given this invitation to our readers, and year after year the response has been increasingly large; and year after year have come letters like this: "Thank you for the light on the Jew first. I want to begin the new year with a gift to the Jew first." And if our letter files could talk, what a story of blessing they could reveal out of the hearts of thousands who took God at His word!

THE DIVINE ARITHMETIC

January, 1927

A handful from a handful leaves a barrelful. "Make me a little cake first," entreated Elijah of the poor widow at Zarephath. "But I only have a handful of meal in a barrel," she had said to him. "And after that's gone, I am going to lay me down and die. How can I give you any?" Never mind, "Fear not ... but make me a little cake *first,* and *after* that make for thee and for thy son."

She could have argued, and refused, or compromised; because, you know, our modern practice seems to be the so-called primitive law of self-preservation. But she did not argue, and she did not refuse, and she did not indulge in sophisticated reasoning. Here is the divine record:—"She went and did according to the saying of Elijah."

And look what happened:—Elijah had promised her, if she would do what he had asked her, "The barrel of meal shall not waste, neither shall the cruse of oil fail, until the day that the Lord sendeth rain upon the earth." 1 Kings 17: 11-16.

And so it was, for we read, "And the barrel of meal wasted not, neither did the cruse of oil fail, according to the word of the Lord, which he spake by Elijah!" In other words there entered into the transaction a third element, invisible except to the eye of faith, the Divine arithmetic. God had put His plus sign over against the poor widow's minus barrel, and lo and behold! the addition became multiplication, and the multiplication reached infinity!

And God has always done that to any of His children who are obedient to His commands. Because what God is, even today, hungering for, is *obedience;* not money. He owns

the earth, the heavens, the stars. But *obedience,* that attribute
of the heart which He has so arranged can only be given Him
of our free will. Now we know that God could have sent the
ravens to feed Elijah; He didn't *need* the widow's few grains
of flour. But He was after something infinitely more valuable
than a handful of flour—He wanted a human soul's obedience. And praise God, He found it.

And then something unexpected occurred, the poor widow
received an extra dividend on her investment with the Lord,
for her son who had been taken sick and died was restored
by God to her. So she learned that a business deal with God
was a highly profitable undertaking.

We suppose our readers have already begun to suspect
what we are getting at. Yes, your suspicions are correct, for
this is January, the first month of the New Year, and again
we want to call to your attention God's divine method for
evangelizing the world—To the Jew first!

Make A Little Cake First

Do you see the striking parallel? God, through the Apostle
Paul has said to the Church, "Give the Gospel to all the world,
but give it to the Jew first!" You only have a little bit of it?
You need it all for yourself? You have to attend to your
denominational machinery first? You have your own wheels
to grind? You have your "world program" to look after?
Fear not! Never mind! Do what I ask you; give the Gospel
"to the Jew first"—Make me a little cake first! After you
have done that, there will be plenty, and more, left for you.
Will you do it?

And oh, the tragedy of it—the Church, now for nearly
nineteen hundred years, deliberately refuses obedience to
God's command.

Now you know God can, if He wants to, resort to supernatural means to convert the Jews right now; just as He could have fed Elijah in other ways than by means of the widow's faith. But He *doesn't* want to. He deliberately asks the Christian Church to exercise this much faith in His promise, by giving *to the Jew first*. And what a blessing He stands ready to pour out, if only we will be obedient! It is Divine Arithmetic ready to operate.

And what a loss has come to the Church when she has disobeyed His command! Has not the meal in the barrel truly become moldy? Do not the tidings of world apostasy startle the child of God? And is it not true that Jewish Christian testimony has so long been kept out of the Church that the very Church has become paganized? How else can you explain the legions of men who are brazenly and blatantly proclaiming their heathenisms from countless pulpits of our land? Could that have been possible in the early days of Apostolic Christianity, when Jewish Christians were in the saddle, and when "To the Jew first" really meant something, and was literally practiced?

They Took God Literally

Oh, for a revival of early Jewish Christianity! Oh, for men and women who will cast aside world philosophies, and denominational fetishes, and turn back to the pure simplicity of primitive Christianity, when those early disciples took what God said *literally*.

Will you do it, dear reader? May we repeat, as tenderly as we know how, the invitation we have given before in these columns?—will you not try God for this year by writing, "to the Jew first," in your missionary program? Year after year each January, we have given this invitation to our readers, and year after year the response has been increasingly large; and year after year have come letters like this: "Thank you for the light on the Jew first: I want to begin the new year with a gift to the Jew first."

How about you? Won't you try it for this year?

THE BLESSING THAT MAKETH POOR

January, 1928

When is a blessing not a blessing? The question may look simple, or even foolish, but upon its proper answer there hinge some far-reaching issues. We ask it, becacse for these many years we have, out of the deepest convictions of our souls, predicated the entire Jewish Mission appeal upon two bed-rock foundations. Upon these two fundamental principles, so far as we are concerned, the Jewish appeal must live or die, and we have been willing to cast our all on their integrity. The first principle is the New Testament order of Gospel promulgation, an order that has never been cancelled by God from the day that Paul enunciated it, to this very hour—"To the Jew First." The other, the second re-enforcing stone in the foundation, is the Old Testament promise given to the first Hebrew, Abraham, at the time God started the nation on its career down the centuries—"I will bless them that bless thee." A sort of red flag of warning to all the world throughout all generations—"For whatever you do unto this people, you will have to settle the account with Me!"

And so we have maintained always that first, the true child of God must give the Gospel to the Jew first; and second, that God will bless such a child of His, in a way that will be definite, clear-cut, and undeniable.

And to these claims of ours have come from time to time some serious protests: "What a mercenary appeal!" gasped some; and others said, "I don't give to God because I want something back!" And still others have been actually lured into the idea that by helping the Jews they have discovered the road to independent wealth, and they have sent money to us with the expectation that God would in return pour out upon them such a shower of gold that they could not contain it. Later, they would write us to complain that they have not gotten the wealth they expected, and were therefore greatly disappointed!

So this brings us down to some real thinking on a manifestly difficult problem. Let us start out with this postulate, that money in itself is not always a blessing. At first look, you might be inclined to question this statement. But open your eyes and look around you, and you will be astonished to see how many cases there are where money has been a curse, and not a blessing. And this brings us to ask for a definition of the word blessing. There are many definitions, each depending on the viewpoint of the one who defines. But we think no true child of God will take issue with us if we define the word blessing to mean any experience, pleasant or unpleasant, propitious or calamitous, which brings us into a closer relation to God our Father. "The greatest blessing that ever came into my life," said a wealthy servant of God to us some few years ago, "was in 1892, when a sudden financial panic swept away my entire fortune, and drove me back to my overalls in my garden. I had slowly accumulated $100,000 and in those days I was considered a wealthy man. But I got far away from God, and my soul was surely and gradually shriveling up. Prosperity had come upon my spiritual being like some slow creeping palsy, and I saw it coming; but like one in a trance, I could not fight it off. Then God took a hand, and took from me every dollar I had; but He gave me back my soul!"

Leanness In The Soul

What may seem to you a blessing may in truth be only a curse in disguise. How do you know that you are competent to judge as to what is best for you? Is your little child better able to know what is good for him than you are? And likewise, who knows better what is good for you—you, or your Heavenly Father? Solemnly have we thought many times of the wilderness experience of the children of Israel. What a tragedy is locked up in the one short sentence of Psalm 106:15, "And He gave them their request; but sent leanness into their soul." *Leanness in the soul!* What a price to pay for the gratification of their desire, a thing which they *thought* would be a blessing. And how much better off they would have been if they had just said, "Oh God, Thou knowest our need far better than we do. Do Thou with us as Thou knowest best!"

So it comes to this: a blessing is not a blessing when it is outside of God's will for us. You want money; but how do you know you can handle the money to His honor? You want Fame; how do you know but Fame will turn your head, and prove your undoing? You want that baby of yours to rise from the sick-bed; instead God takes the child to Himself. You murmur; but how do you know whether that child may not have grown up to be a disgrace to you, and to bring your white hairs down to an early grave? How do you know? God knows! And you can safely trust Him to do what is for your best good, if you are doing His will, and obeying His leading.

And the only place you can take in relation to Him, is the place Job took, when he said, "Though *He slay me,* yet will I trust in Him." Such a sublime faith can be happy and blessed under any kind of physical trials or surroundings. It is told that Spurgeon once called on a farmer, and saw on the fantail of the weather-vane on the barn-roof the words painted "God is love." Spurgeon, surprised, asked, "Why did you put that there? Did you mean that God's love is as changeable as the wind?" And the farmer answered, "No, indeed; what I mean is, that no matter which way the wind blows, God is love."

Our dear friend, Dr. W. B. Hinson, now with the Lord, wrote once a striking sentence which stuck like a Scotch burr to our memory: "The God who gave Jesus Christ to die for you, cannot hurt you!" And it will help us all incalculably if even in the midst of sorrow and anguish and bitterness of soul, we will repeat to ourselves that sentence, "The God who gave Jesus Christ to die for you, cannot hurt you."

Pleasing Our Heavenly Father

And so we are more sure than ever that if you will do as God has told you concerning giving the Gospel "To the Jew first" there will come into your life a new and a definite blessing; because you will know you are in His will. Not because you want money reward! But because you want to please Him! A manufacturer told us a few years ago, "You know, I started to help your mission only because I wanted to test out the promise, 'I will bless them that bless thee,' and I have never made so much money in my life as since I started helping the Jews. It works! And wherever you go, you should tell people that." And we replied, "We are truly sorry for your motive, because it is not sound, nor Scriptural; how do you know that financial prosperity is going to be a blessing to you? Suppose in God's wisdom He should see fit to take away your money; would you then curse God and say He failed to keep His promises?" Our friend made no reply to that, but said only, "You have given me something to think about."

Once more it is January, the beginning of a new year—how fast these Januaries come and go! And for many Januaries past we have invited you to start for the new year a new way—God's way—"To the Jew first."

And now again we open the door and give you the invitation, "Do God's work in God's way—to the Jew first." Israel is fast rushing into her day of reckoning yonder in Armageddon, for God has a controversy to settle with Israel. So there is not much time left, and all the more important it becomes for the Church to give, while there is yet time, her testimony, "To the Jew First," for the night soon cometh, when no man works, a black night for Israel, but a glorious morning for sunrise for the Church.

FIRST IN CONDEMNATION

January, 1929

It happened in a mid-western town several years ago. The writer was to preach at the evening service. The Pastor began his introduction of the speaker by reading a few verses from the second chapter of Romans. When he finished the 8th verse, he stopped for a short rhetorical pause, or possibly to get his breath; then, with a half turn of his head towards us, he proceeded to read the 9th verse, with solemn emphasis on each word,

"Tribulation and anguish, upon every soul of man that doeth evil, of the Jew first, and also of the Gentile."

Then he closed the Book, and announced the writer to speak!

We arose, and as affably as we could, we said, "Your pastor, in his haste to introduce us, must have forgotten to finish the beautiful Scripture lesson, for he stopped just one verse too soon. May we read to you the next verse also?"

And we read the 10th verse, also the 11th, and tried to give each word as powerful an emphasis as he had given to the 9th verse:

"But glory, honour, and peace, to every man that worketh good, to the Jew first, and also to the Gentile: For there is no respect of persons with God."

And that experience has stayed with us ever since. And many times have we pondered over its significance. For that pastor, as good and kindly a man of God as ever drew breath, unintentionally, and wholly unconsciously, revealed what is too generally true even in this day, of many thousands of God's people all over the land—that a mental attitude exists in the average Gentile Christian consciousness which seems perfectly willing to give the Jew all the tribulation that is coming to him, but begrudges the same Jew any possible compensating consideration. Witness, for instance, the ready ease with which so many of the present day expounders of Scripture assign to the Jews all the curses and punishments prophesied for Israel and Jerusalem, and with just as ready and compunctionless ease appropriate to themselves as Christians all the blessings prophesied in the Old Testament for the very same Israel and the very same Jerusalem! In other words, the principle that seems to be followed is that if you find a blessing promised in the Old Testament, to Israel, it must of necessity mean the Church; but if you find a curse in the Old Testament, promised to the same Israel, let's give it to the Jew, he is welcome to it!

But notice how eminently fair and just God is: In the verses we have quoted, Romans 2:9-11, He gives us a complete and satisfying exposition of the doctrine we have for so many years presented to our readers "To the Jew First." What He tells us in these verses is so crystal clear that we marvel how any right minded Christian can ever resent the divine program of "to the Jew First" as being unfair. God tells us here as plainly as language can be made to talk, that the Jew will be the first one to receive judgment and punishment at God's hand, and this punishment will be "indignation and wrath, tribulation and anguish," an awful visitation to contemplate.

It is only after the Jewish nation has received this "double for all her sins" that the Gentiles shall come into their judgment.

God's Principle

So God is laying down in Romans a principle of compensatory justice; if this poor Jewish nation is to be plunged *first* at the close of the present dispensation, into the unspeakable darkness of the time of Jacob's trouble, then by all the laws of fairness this same nation should be placed *first* in the present age of grace, an age when the Gospel is being promulgated the wide world over. And strangely enough, God backs up all of this arrangement by this astounding sentence, "for there is no respect of persons with God." How many times have our friends tried to refute the scriptural doctrine "to the Jew first" by quoting the very verse just given, "for there is no respect of persons with God." But you can well imagine their astonishment when we have immediately turned to that verse in Scripture and compelled such a friend to read the two preceding verses, that is, Romans 2:9 and 10; for they discovered at once that this declaration of God's impartiality, given at the very place where God declares the doctrine of "to the Jew First," must have a different meaning from what they thought it had. To any open and logical mind, the meaning is certainly clear enough. It means fundamentally that God is no respecter of persons; therefore it must follow logically that since God is no respecter of persons He could not possibly plan to give tribulation and anguish "to the Jew first" without also planning to give "glory, honor and peace" likewise "to the Jew first."

First in condemnation, first in grace; this is all that is meant by the present Gospel dispensation and program of God, "to the Jew First." If the Jew is going to suffer unspeakable tortures in the time of the great tribulation *first,* then let us have the kindness of heart and the decency of fair play to give now in the present age of grace, the Gospel "to the Jew first." It is only a few months ago that a friend of ours took violent exception to this doctrine, and we proceeded at once to present to him the arguments that we are writing in these columns. "I never saw that before," he exclaimed, "and that settles the whole matter for me. Now I am completely satisfied. I always thought that it was purely a selfish conceit on the part of the Jewish Christian, but now I see it is only God's fairness and justice."

And the writer hopes that many of our readers will go over these lines, readers perhaps who have until now not seen eye to eye with us on this point, but who from now on will be able to say with the friend alluded to, "I am now satisfied."

It is again a new year, and again a first month of a new year, and so again we open the doors of invitation to all of our friends and say to you, "Let's do for this year God's work in God's way, to the Jew first." And having done it God's way, we shall all be satisfied for we shall have done that which is pleasing in His sight.

IS THIS A GENTILE CHURCH AGE?

January, 1930

Sometimes a consideration of a negative helps to establish the truth of a positive. Strange as it may seem, in spite of the fact that nothing is stated in Scripture more unequivocally than the clear cut instruction that the Church owes the Gospel "To the Jew First," there are many of God's children even to this day who resent bitterly the very mention of such a Scripture truth. Just why a child of God should become so angry when we speak of God's place for the Jew in the present age, we cannot comprehend; unless it be that the Evil One is desperately busy in these last days to thwart God's plans, and is blinding the very children of light to this exceedingly vital truth.

But suppose, just for the sake of considering the negative, we assume that the New Testament order, "To the Jew First," was not at all operative, and we will suppose, as some teachers would have us believe, that this is preeminently a "Gentile Church" age. Then what would be the inevitable implications?

1st. We would be forced to conclude that God had not only reversed Himself but had become vindictive. "God is love" would be only a mockery. And the clear declaration of the Lord Jesus Christ, that "whosoever will" may come, would only be a misleading statement, for it would have to say also, "except the Jew!" That God was so resentful because the Jewish *Nation* as such rejected Him, that He passed a curse upon every *individual* Jew for all time, to make it impossible for such a Jew to become a child of God through faith in the Lord Jesus Christ! You see, it needs only to show the logical sequence of such a theory to show its monstrosity.

2nd. We would be compelled to forfeit the benefits accru-
ing to us by virtue of the fact that the *first* Christians were
all Jews, the *first* Church was all Jewish, the *first* missionaries
were all Jews, the first martyrs were Jews, the first Bishop
of the Christian Church, was a Jew—James. Certainly, if
these, all Jews, had no right to the Gospel, "To the Jew
First," then they were out of place; and if they were usurp-
ing prerogatives not theirs, then their faith, their testimony,
all are suddenly proven to be of no value, and the Christian
Church suddenly finds herself on a foundation of sand! For
you have no right to lay claim to a fraud, and you cannot
build a structure of Christian dogma upon an invalid premise.

Modern Churches Without Jews

3rd. You would deprive the Church of Christ of Jewish-
Christian testimony for all of these two thousand years. And,
barring out such testimony most naturally means a gradual
ignoring and a final denial of all those things which God had
taught the Jew to be indispensable in his relation to Himself;
we mean such basic doctrines as blood atonement, the Passover type, the Davidic Throne. Who but a Jew can best ex-
pound and exemplify these precious truths to an unbelieving
and sophisticated Gentile mass? And, indeed, is it not start-
lingly true that as the Church has become increasingly paganized through the persistent teaching and practice of the unscriptural and pernicious "Gentile Church" theory, the spread
of apostasy has gone on in almost algebraic ratios? Do you
know, for instance, of any appreciable number of Jewish
Christians who retain membership in modernistic churches?
Indeed not, for the Jewish Christian knows full well the
meaning of the Virgin birth, the vicarious atonement, the
blood sacrifice, and the hundred other Bible doctrines so dear
to the true child of God. The question is quite pertinent,

therefore, as to whether the Church has not brought upon herself her own punishment by deliberately following a no-Jew, all-Gentile practice.

4th. You would render impossible the return of our Lord to earth. For it was to the Jews He said, "Ye shall not see me henceforth until ye shall say, blessed is He that cometh in the Name of the Lord!" Matt. 23:29. Yes, dear reader, whether we will or no, His coming back to earth actually hinges on Jewish conversion. And if there is no "to the Jew first" practice by the Church in the present day, it means only that the Jew is to be left in crass, dense ignorance of the Gospel; and since ignorance is progressive, the Jew would thus be driven farther and farther from the Lord Jesus Christ.

And so we could go on, and prove point by point, the utter absurdity of such a premise. But we have said enough to satisfy any right-minded child of God of the folly of the "Gentile Church" theory, and the inevitable necessity of a strict obedience to the Scripture method of world evangelization—"To the Jew First." To any real Christian we need to say no more. A "Thus saith the Lord" is enough to His obedient child.

And the writer hopes that many of our dear readers will go over these lines, readers perhaps who have until now not seen eye to eye with us on this point, but who from now on will be able to say, "I am now satisfied."

ALSO TO THE GENTILES

January, 1931

An astonishing thing had happened in Jerusalem. Peter was telling the Jewish disciples about it. It was nothing less than that God had given him a clear summons to preach the Gospel to the Gentiles, as well as to the Jews. This command was a shock to Peter's plans for the Kingdom of God. Up to this point it had not been revealed to him that there was to be a Church hiatus before the Throne of David would be re-established in Jerusalem. "Wilt thou at this time restore the Kingdom to Israel?" was the question the first Jewish disciples had asked of our Lord just before His ascension. And our Lord answered them by saying, "This is really not your business; but you are to be my witnesses, first in Jerusalem, next in Judea, next in Samaria, and then to the uttermost parts of the world."

And now Peter finally obeyed the special vision which God had given him, and he had gone to the Gentiles, and his first experiences brought to him only astonishment. He actually found that God was beginning to gather out a remnant from among the Gentiles just as He was gathering out the elect from among the Jewish nation. And the testimony of the Scripture is "And they of the circumcision which believed were astonished ... because that on the Gentiles also was poured out the gift of the Holy Ghost." Acts 10:45.

Later on Peter tells this story to a gathering of Jewish believers, some of whom were inclined to resent the thought that Gentiles were to become partakers with the Jews in the spiritual blessings of the Abrahamic covenant. But after Peter had finished his story and told of the unmistakable leadings and workings of God, we come across a most illuminating and remarkable statement concerning these early simple-minded and faith-filled Jewish believers. "When they heard these things, they held their peace, and glorified God, saying, Then hath God also to the Gentiles granted repentance unto life!" Acts 11:18.

Have You Returned The Compliment?

First, astonishment; second, joy. They had not expected nor had believed it possible for a Gentile to become a child of God, for they had looked upon the Gentiles for many centuries past with a hopelessness of despair. But now God was actually working among the Gentiles, and once they really understood this remarkable fact, you will notice that they changed their attitude completely, threw aside willingly all the prejudice of the many centuries before, and then glorified God. In other words they welcomed the Gentile believers with open arms, and rejoiced that these were to be made fellow-heirs with them of salvation through the precious blood of the Lord Jesus Christ.

What a vast amount of food for thought is to be found in these incidents for the true child of God who is seeking earnestly and sincerely to do His will, and how wonderfully transformed would be the Church of Christ today if only she would study afresh these elementary facts concerning the beginnings of the Gospel days.

First, notice the rather strange contrast between the attitude of those early Jewish disciples toward the Gentiles who had been their implacable enemies and tormentors and slave-drivers, and the attitude of the present day Church towards the problem of the Jewish believer and towards the problem of preaching the Gospel to the Jew. A study of this situation alone in our own country will reveal a situation that would shame any Christian who makes the least pretense to understanding the Word of God and to possessing in his own heart the love of the Lord Jesus Christ.

In a church not many hundred miles away from New York, hardly a year ago, a brilliant young Jew was taken in for baptism. The pastor happened to be a lover of God's covenant people, Israel, and was elated over the privilege of actually baptizing a Jewish believer. But no sooner was this done, than a wave of protest and prejudice made itself felt throughout the church, and the pastor was severely criticized for having had the presumption to baptize a Jew into the membership of that proud, wealthy and self-satisfied church. One of our own workers had been instrumental in the conversion of this young Jew, and this worker was an eye witness to all that had occurred.

A Pastor Defies His Deacons

In another city in the middlewest, a pastor had faithfully labored with a prominent Jew over a period of many months, and finally that Jew was brought under the conviction of the Holy Spirit, and asked this pastor to baptize him. The pastor announced at the prayer meeting that the following Sunday night he was to have a new experience, one that had never come to him before; he was going to baptize a Jewish believer upon his public confession of faith in the Lord Jesus Christ. After the prayer meeting was over a committee of church members waited upon the pastor and told him point blank that if he baptized any Jew in that church it would mean that he must resign from the pastorate, and that they were ready to force his resignation. But the pastor had a will power born of the Holy Spirit and he defied this committee and told them that on the following Sunday night he was going to baptize this Jew, even if it were the last act he would ever do as pastor of the church. He did baptize the

Jew and the Jew became a stalwart pillar in the church, but imagine the feelings of that poor Jew when he found himself among a people where instead of warm Christian fellowship, there was an undercurrent of hatred, suspicion and prejudice.

Obvious Hypocrisy

But, the early Jewish disciples glorified God when to the Gentiles also had been given the Holy Spirit. And this brings us to our second reflection. It centers itself about the expression "the Gentiles also." Again we have a startling contrast between the attitude of those early Jewish believers, and the attitude of some of our present day so-called Christian leaders. There is, for instance, one prominent Christian leader in America, and he has a few who seem to swallow without question what he says, whose constant shibboleth is "This is not the time for the Jews, this is only the time for the Gentiles. It is my opinion and it is my judgment that Jewish Mission work in the present age is a failure." As though this leader's "opinion" is worth a grain of salt as compared with the teaching of God's Word! Of course Jewish Mission work will be a failure wherever such "leaders" emit vociferously their opinions to that effect, and then proceed to act out in their own lives these very opinions! We wonder, for instance, how much such a one has ever done personally to bring one Jewish soul to the knowledge of the Lord Jesus Christ. We are sure that if he had engaged himself even in the smallest degree to an honest Jewish missionary effort, he could never say that Jewish missionary work is a failure.

Of course, all of this finds its roots in the sad fact that many even of God's choicest saints have grossly misunderstood the purpose of God in the present age. They have either ignorantly or deliberately misconstrued the expression used in Scripture, "the times of the Gentiles," and in other parts of Scripture a similar expression, which is really identical, "the fulness of the Gentiles." The error has been to apply the expression, "the times of the Gentiles," to the Church age, instead of to the world governments. So far as the Church is concerned there is no such thing as "the times of the Gentiles." This is the Church age in which Jews "and Gentiles also" are being called out by God through the operation of the Holy Spirit, to form His body, the Church, which when complete, will bring about His return for the Church. It is always *the Church,* and it is never, the Gentile Church. The very word Church means, called out, and the calling out then must be from among all nations; but see how careful the Word of God is, for it says distinctly that this calling out process is as from the Jew first, and from the Gentiles ALSO.

Rough-Shod Lawlessness

And strange it is to witness the perversity of human nature. No sooner are the Gentiles in the Church saddle, than they ride roughshod over Jews, over Scripture, over divine precept, over sentiment, over common gratitude. And we are called upon to witness the complete reversal of God's program, so that instead of the order being "To the Jew first and also to the Greek," it has become, "To the Gentile first, last and always!"

But thanks be to God, He never, in the worst days of apostasy in ages past, has been without His faithful remnant. Sometimes, as was the case with Enoch, or Abraham, the remnant has been woefully small, but it was a remnant. And a remnant of even one, is a great big remnant, if God is there! So now, the God of Israel, the covenant-keeping God, has a remnant even in these days of darkness and confusion. And this remnant is determined, above all else, to do His will, for they realize that after all there is nothing in the world so important as the doing of His will.

So, "To the Jew first" has become the fixed and blessed practice of many of His choicest children, and they have given us abundant testimony as to God's blessing upon them for such a faithful obedience.

Even as we write these lines there comes a letter from a generous friend of the Mission, which says, "This is the eleventh time I have sent to the Jewish Mission and I am free to say I get more kick out of this than that which I hand over to the .... Church, which amount is considerably more."

What the dear brother put in the rather picturesque language of the day, really was intended by him to mean that he received more spiritual blessings from the gifts that he makes to the Jewish Mission work than from any other interest that he has in the Lord's harvest field; the truth is, that this is exactly as it should be, and this is what we have been trying to put before our friends for these many years. It is only the working out of God's unchangeable and unimpeachable law. You may put it down as an irrevocable axiom, just as true and just as sure as are the stars in their courses, that you cannot put your hands upon the Jew for good, without God paying you back, with interest. When you associate yourself with the Jewish Mission enterprise, you are literally transacting business with God in such a way and in such a close contact with Him, that there is nothing else in the wide world to compare with it. All that this statement needs as to verification is that you put it to the test, in your own personal life, for one year.

And so, this January, at the beginning of the year,

which holds such possibilities of tremendous destinies as to God's program, we open wide the doors of invitation to our friends. Let's give the Gospel, even more intensely than ever before, in God's way—"To the Jew First!"

Try it on our recommendation for one year!

THE CONSTANT "UNTIL"

January, 1932

A challenging letter reached us some time ago. It was from a friend who questioned the validity of setting signs and dates for our Lord's return. "Show me one passage in the Bible," the friend wrote, "which definitely states that after a certain number of people are converted, His body is thus made complete and the Church caught up!"

And as we pondered the point raised in this brother's letter, some new rays of light began to pour in upon us, and we began more and more to understand the clear differentiation which the Lord has made as between the Jewish nation and the Church. To the Church, because it is a spiritual body, walking by faith, He perforce would give no signs. To the Jews, however, His earthly people, who had always walked by sight, He did always give signs.

With this clue we followed on, and finally sent to our brother a reply, the essence of which we feel would be helpful to our readers at this time, because it reveals particularly illuminating truth concerning the doctrine so often stressed in our columns, a doctrine having to do with the plan of God for Gospel proclamation in the present Church age—"To the Jew First." So here are the important paragraphs of the letter, and we will follow these paragraphs with a few further ones to show the application to the doctrine of the Gospel "to the Jew First":

We have felt that the coming of the Lord Jesus Christ was rather definitely conditioned upon the conversion of the Jews, or at least the conversion of a sufficient number of them to justify the technical statement that the Jewish nation has accepted Christ. By technical I mean that just as the Lord had promised to restore the Jews from the Babylonian captivity back to their own land, and yet when the restoration took place hardly fifty thousand were returned, yet these were sufficient to justify the technical fulfillment of God's promise.

Our basis for such a conviction is to be found in a passage like Matt. 23: 39,

"Ye shall not see me henceforth until ye shall say, Blessed is he that cometh in the name of the Lord."

This passage has always meant to us just what it says, that is, literally, that whenever the Jews should turn to the Lord Jesus Christ, He would have to appear. The "until" in this case, I think you will agree, must carry with it a continuing condition, otherwise the statement of the Lord Jesus Christ is impeached.

The Promise Is Conditional

It is in the light of this original premise that the statement of the Holy Spirit through Peter on the day of Pentecost is to be explained, Acts 3: 19, 20. R. V.

"Repent ye therefore and be converted that your sins may be blotted out, *that so* may come times of refreshing from the presence of the Lord, and he shall send Jesus Christ which before was preached unto you."

Thus again you have a conditioned promise, and again to us it has always been a matter of conviction that if the Jews on that very day when Peter preached the sermon had in sufficient numbers accepted Christ, He would have returned instantly.

Following now through to the missionary activities of Paul, we find the same note of conditional prediction. Romans 11: 13-15 says:

"For I speak to you Gentiles, inasmuch as I am the apostle of the Gentiles, I magnify mine office; if by any means I may provoke to emulation them which are my flesh, and might save some of them. For if the casting away of them be the reconciling of the world, what shall the receiving of them be, but life from the dead?"

Evidently to Paul had been given the same revelation, that just as soon as the Jews were converted it would mean "life from the dead," for undoubtedly such conversion would mean the coming of the Lord, and that would mean of course that through the Jewish nation the entire world would be brought to Christ. It is the same thought again in Romans 9: 1, 2 and 3, and certainly the statement in the 3d verse is so powerful and drastic as to stagger the mind: for the statement reads,

"For I could wish that myself were accursed from Christ for my brethren, my kinsmen according to the flesh."

Such a burning passion cannot reasonably be ascribed merely to motives of patriotism, for the Holy Spirit is very careful in the first verse to say clearly, "my conscience bearing me witness in the Holy Ghost."

Finally, following out the same argument we look for a moment at the closing scene in the divine record of the life of Paul, Acts 28: 30, 31. Here you have a remarkable situation in that only two verses before, Paul had declared to the Jews that since they would not hear the Gospel he would go to the Gentiles. Yet the very closing verse of this chapter reads that Paul remained in Rome,

"preaching the kingdom of God, and teaching those things which concern the Lord Jesus Christ."

In other words we take it that Paul was still giving out a two-fold message, the first part of the message was "the

Kingdom of God" which had to do of course with the restoration of the Jews to their own land and the establishing of the Kingdom, if they (the Jews) would accept Him; the second clause of this two-fold work of Paul, we take to mean that side by side with the Kingdom message was also the Gospel of grace, so that souls would be saved from time to time even though the Jews as a nation would not avail themselves of the constantly open opportunity to accept Christ and to hasten His coming.

The "Until" Not Repealed

Thus endeth the letter to our brother. There remains now to add a few further words, because as our friends know, we have in January of the past few years tried to present in these columns, always from a slightly different angle, the importance in God's plan of the true followers of the Lord Jesus Christ obeying the divine missionary order, "to the Jew first." What we would add further is only to say that in view of the unrepealed "until" of Matthew 23: 29, it is still true at the present day that if the Jewish nation, or a sufficient number of them, should accept Christ, He would come. Thus the divine order, "To the Jew First" takes on a powerful significance, for in no other way can the Church of Christ hasten the coming of our Lord more rapidly than by evangelizing the Jewish nation, speedily, persistently, and extensively, to the uttermost parts of the earth. More and more, as the age seems to be drawing to a close, God is stirring up increasing numbers of His children, to a new sense of the imperative of this Jewish Gospel program; perhaps this stirring up process can be rightly compared to those other days, nineteen hundred years ago, when the wise men were stirred up, no doubt by the direct leading of God, to notice the wonderful sign of the Star which slowly but surely led them to the place where the Christ-child lay. Perhaps we are nearer a reenactment of similar experiences in these latter days, only that the scenery has been shifted. That some of the choicest of the Lord's people who in these days of distress and great personal want find it in their hearts to deny themselves further and give for the speedy evangelizing of the Jews, and consider that that is even more important than their own bread and butter, surely this is a sign of God's leading which will bear comparison with the sign of the Star which led the wise men on their holy mission nineteen hundred years ago. No child of God could possibly sit in our place, and read the letters that come to us without a profound sense of the supernatural interference of God in these days of apostasy. Just read a few of these letters, and see if they do not stir your heart to its depths, as they have stirred our hearts:

"Though our business is in the hands of a receiver, to be sold tomorrow, I felt that I must send something. Hence the small check which I enclose. Personally, I feel that our debt to the Jews is greater than we can ever pay."

"My heart is strangely touched towards the Jews. I have always been praying for them—since I understood their relation to God—but lately I feel more than ever a desire to help them in some way. I am enclosing what might seem a very tiny sum—but almost everything I have seems going or gone—yet I must help the Jews. If God reveals His mercy to me and I can send more—later on—you will certainly hear from me."

"I am very sure it was no man or the teaching of any man that has made me debtor to this work. It was the Lord himself who has revealed it to me in His Word, and has enabled me in this depression to have that I may give. So it is all of grace."

"It doesn't seem long since I wrote you a letter similar to this, in which I said I was going to follow my Saviour's command 'To the Jew First' and that is just what I am doing now in the closing hours of this old year, sending you a little to help carry the Gospel to them for whom it was first sent, and because they then refused it, by grace I have received it. This will be the first thing I do on the New Year, start this letter in the mail to you. The Lord's blessing can't be bought with a price, but I believe He will reward obedience, and if some one or more are blessed through this little gift, that will be MY reward."

"And Also To The Greek"

And so, throughout these years of labor in our Jewish work, there has grown up a most beautiful custom among our friends, a custom which to the best of our knowledge was first given public prominence by the sainted Hudson Taylor, of China Inland Mission fame. It was Mr. Taylor's great joy on the first day of January of each year, from far off China, to send a contribution to the greatly honored Mr. John Wilkinson of London, and on the check Mr. Taylor would write, "To the Jew First." Not to be outdone by this literal obedience to the Word of God, Mr. Wilkinson quaintly enough, would send a personal check of his own to Mr. Hudson Taylor for the China Inland Mission, and would cross the check with the words, "And also to the Greek."

And so each year many, many of our friends have chosen the month of January in which to send a special gift for the work of this Mission, "To the Jew First," and by doing so they have replenished our treasury in such abundance that we were able to go forward with plans for the entire year, knowing that the Lord already had given us an earnest of the support that would come during the next eleven months, and that we need go forward without fear or misgiving.

Thus again, for this year, we open the door of invitation to our friends, and say to each of you, "Come in, partake of the feast of the blessing prepared for you and all who delight to do His will." For surely there is blessing waiting for the child of God who will once more put Him to the test; a new year, a new plan, "To the Jew First," and you are thus a partner with Him in the carrying out of His everlasting purposes from before the foundation of the world.

SHEARING SAMSON'S LOCKS

January, 1933

Even in the dark hour of world depression, may we express to you, every one of our dear friends, our earnest wishes and prayers for a New Year permeated with the joy of His presence, so that your experience shall be that of Psalm 30:5, "Weeping may endure for a night, but joy cometh in the morning." And if it should so be that before this year rolls away into eternity, we who are His shall have heard the sound of the trump and have been suddenly caught up to be with Him forever, what a morning of joy that will be!

We are taking more than the space usually allotted to our January article this time because of our conviction as to its importance in helping the child of God to understand some recent rather bewildering events. For the Church of Christ has been betrayed; and betrayed in the house of those who profess to be her friends: and Satan rejoices.

There is an organization, as our readers must know, which calls itself "The Federal Council of Churches of Christ in America," and which boasts, but quite untruthfully, that it represents 20,000,000 Christians in America. This organization seems to aspire to the position of a perpetual and international Mr. Fixit. It dabbles in everything under the sun, and has a finger in every pie. It creates committees, and commissions, and investigations, and researches, and conferences, and throws out to the world its solemn pronouncements upon all and sundry subjects conceivable, with the finality of a pontifical encyclical.

For several years its titular head was the Rev. S. Parkes Cadman, D.D. This is the Dr. Cadman who now conducts a syndicated newspaper column entitled "Everyday Questions," in which column he has repeatedly and frankly asserted that he is opposed to "proselyting"; that if you are a Jew, be a good Jew, and you'll get to heaven; if you are a Catholic, be a good Catholic and all will be well. Of course any ten year old child knows that this is treacherously false, but popularity is popularity.

In more recent days, the President of this "Federal Council of Churches of Christ in America" has been the well known Bishop Francis J. McConnell, of the Methodist Episcopal Church. Bishop McConnell last year presided at a specially arranged meeting in one of the Methodist Churches in New York, on the night of the Jewish New Year. The purpose was to pay a compliment to the Jews, and to tell them how important they were. Taking part, and sitting on the platform, among others, aside from Bishop McConnell, were a Jewish Christ-rejecting Rabbi, a woman Theosophist leader, a Mohammedan-worshipping Arab and a lawyer known for his Communistic sympathies. All these joined together in a "unity of religions" meeting, and each praised the other's religion as being so fine. But we noticed that when the Jewish Rabbi expatiated on the glories of the Jews' future in Palestine, the Arab was not quite so happy about it; for soon after, the Arab took his turn at the flattery business, but instead of flattering the Rabbi, he practically told him that the Jews should mind their own business and keep out of Palestine, which belonged by right to the Arabs! And right there the "unity" was terribly stretched—dangerously near the snapping point!

Well, we have digressed, but, may we hope, for the enlightenment of our readers? What we started out to tell you was that in recent days two important pieces of treachery to the Lord Jesus Christ have been perpetrated on the Church, and it is necessary that the children of light shall have their eyes opened and be fully warned as to the significance of these startling occurrences. May it not be that just as Delilah betrayed Samson and finally robbed him of his secret power, so the unbelievers of the present generation have leaped into the saddles of the Christian organizations of our country, and are determined similarly to rob the Church of her power? Is it not true that the secret power which the Lord gave to the Church of Christ is to be found in the fact of the Holy Spirit? And is it not true that the attacks that have been made in recent years upon the Church of Christ have been with the one objective of removing the Holy Spirit from His place, and substituting a materialistic and rationalistic system of religion?

The First Betrayal

We find such an attack in an article which appears in the "B'Nai B'Rith Magazine" of March, 1931, on page 192. The article is entitled "Are Christian Missions Menacing Judaism?" It is written by a gentleman by the name of Rev. Everett R. Clinchy, who bears the imposing title of "Secretary, Committee of Good Will between Jews and Christians, Federal Council of Churches of Christ in America." In this article Mr. Clinchy himself tells us, "I am a Presbyterian Minister in good and regular standing." Here are a few paragraphs from the article which will give you the gist of the discussion:

"But why does the Christian missionary feel compelled to approach the Jews? Has not the Jew the Bible, the testaments of the patriarchs, the teachings of Hillel, the writings of later rabbis, a knowledge of Laotze, Confucius, Gautama, Jesus, and all other lives? Added to the normal cultural impetus, the Christian missionary to the Jew has the conviction (sometimes bordering on the pathological) that he has the only way of salvation. This is what missionaries mean by their duty to preach the news about that one way. Put most naively, as the story is in Green Pastures, mankind went wild some time after God made Adam and Eve, and God started all over again by sending a flood and saving only two of every kind. Still man chose evil more often than good. God pleaded with them through the prophets. Many of the prophets the people killed. Then God despaired over man, and for a time God ignored the earth. Finally, however, this merciful God decided that he had not done enough, and so God sacrificed his Son, that whosoever should believe in him should have everlasting life. The Christian missionary, if he believes this promise, says to God, like Gabriel in Marc Connelly's drama, 'O. K. Lawd!' And so the missionaries have gone out into all the world. The one who believes in supernatural Christology couches his creed in more sophisticated terms, to be sure, but the fact is that *he believes it,* and he feels that it would be a sin not to go about telling everybody about the Gospel. There are missionaries pleading with Oxford University unbelievers, Chinese students, Gandhi's followers, Unitarians in the United States, primitive Samoans, distinguished Japanese leaders, Modernist Baptists, and Jews, to mention only a few categories. I have a missionary friend who writes to me from China; he is praying for my conversion to his particular Christology. (I am a Presbyterian minister in good and regular standing.) The missionary approach is not an insult, as some Jews believe; it is a state of mind.

"Does the Good Will movement prepare the way for proselyting? Just the opposite. Good will is an antidote for proselyting. As Christian Sunday Schools learn what Jewish prayers are like—what Jewish homes, and religious schools, and places of worship are doing toward American character building, does anyone suppose that they will want to destroy Judaism? Not a bit of it! These children will grow up a generation which will respect Jews as Jews. Again, as church young people's societies examine their prejudices, call in a Jewish leader in towns all over the country, and these Christian young people learn what ideals, what earnest efforts for good living, what philanthropies, and what an intelligent and powerful religion Jews possess, does anyone think that these Christian young people will want to ask Jews to give up their Judaism? Not by a long sea-mile!"

Certainly this is shocking, and we think little more need be said than just to print the actual fact. The point that this Presbyterian minister "in good and regular standing" wishes us to understand is that anyone who undertakes Jewish Mission work is suffering from a state of mind that borders on the pathological! And there have been trusting Christian people who have actually believed that the Committee of Good Will between Jews and Christians, of the Federal Council of the Churches of Christ in America, was an effort to bring the Jews to Christ!

The Second Betrayal

Thus, having now witnessed this astounding piece of treason as regards the evangelizing of the Jews, it was not a very great step, and certainly it was only logical, for us to expect to witness before long, the same attitude in the realms of the Church's obligation to the heathen. And surely enough, the Christian world has been recently treated to one of the most devastating denouéments that it has experienced in fully a thousand years. It has taken this country almost by storm. We refer to the recently and widely published reports and criticisms put out by a certain Appraisal Committee which seems to have been sponsored by another group called the

Laymen's Foreign Mission Inquiry. It seems that several years ago a group of men got together and, as the *New York Times* reports it, financed largely by Rockefeller money, determined to make a first hand "investigation" of foreign missions. Who these men are and what is their relation to faith in the Word of God, we are not informed. But the main point is, that they have now given to the world their "report" and again we see the spectacle of the Holy Spirit being ruled out of the Foreign Mission enterprise, and a *form* of godliness substituted, without the power of revealed truth.

We are told that the Christian missionary on the foreign field must not press the Gospel of the Lord Jesus Christ as the only way of salvation. Christianity must no longer make quarrel with the other religions of the East. To quote further from a summary review contained in "The Literary Digest":

"Christianity must make cause with the other religions against a common foe . . . the materialism of which Marx, Lenin and Russell are the Arch Priests. It must no longer make appeal for heaven through fear of hell. It must promote heaven here on earth instead of deferring hope beyond the grave. The 'heathen Chinee' to borrow a phrase no longer current in hymn or prayer, is not eternally damned because he knows not Christ. He is one of God's children too. What has the West done that it should be the teacher of mankind?

"There is no ground for a renewed appeal for the support . . . of these Missions in their present form and on their present basis."

Another writer in a recent review on this report, says:

"This is a shot at the very foundations of our Missionary efforts. . . . It becomes evident that the Appraisal Committee of the Laymen's Foreign Mission Inquiry has a type of mind that thinks of the supernatural as superstition, and conceives that the function of religion is in completing the unfinished world view of science. . . . This is a survey of missionaries from the humanist standpoint, and as such it is antagonistic to all evangelical conception."

Mrs. Caroline Atwater Mason gives also a review of this Committee's report and ends with this ominous comment:

"As we lay them down a shadow seems to fall across these Appraisal sheets. Can it be the shadow of a devitalized Christianity?"

Yes, dear sister, it is not only the shadow of a devitalized Christianity, but it is Delilah shearing the locks of Samson. It is Satan working his masterpiece of accomplishing the unpardonable sin, the sin against the Holy Ghost, eliminating the Holy Spirit from the realm of the supernaturally established Church of Christ, and enthroning in its place a materialistic anti-Christian world philosophy.

The Price Of Tolerance

Nor need even our easy-going middle-of-the-road orthodox preachers and laymen be surprised at these developments, for they are just as logical as the statement that two and two make four. When hardly fifty years ago the ugly head of higher criticism and its later sister, which we call today Modernism, but which should be more honestly called just plain infidelity—when this two-headed monster finally was revealed, and a new generation was growing up under the new teaching that the Word of God was full of mistakes, we were only sowing the wind. And just as surely as night follows day, we have now reached a point where we are reaping the whirlwind. The pity is that these poor deluded "tolerant" Christian leaders and laymen followed right along like so many sheep and helped forward the infidelity by passing on millions of dollars for these men to use with shrewd prodigality in the building up of colleges, and universities, and hospitals and schools of science among these heathen nations; thus they intrenched themselves in such a way that now the mischief is done, and they cannot be ousted.

All of this is in accord with a carefully worked out program, and we have only seen the beginning of what is going to happen in the days to come. It is the whole world getting ready for that great Prince that is to come, the Antichrist! And what fodder for infidels, and what joy to Christ-haters, all of these developments bring!

Now to the honest child of God who reads these lines, may we say with the fervor and intensity of the man who is trying to get out of a burning building, "Child of God, awake!"

Has not the time come for scuttling the ship, for a clean separation from those who are dishonoring the Word of God? What right have you as God's child to help forward a machine that is designed to destroy forever all faith in the Lord Jesus Christ? A machinery that tells us that the religions of Hinduism, Buddhism, Shintoism and Confucianism, are all to be placed side by side with Christianity and then the whole mass melted into one fusion that shall produce a religion for all! Can the God and Father of the Lord Jesus Christ be the God of Hinduism? What a shocking and blasphemous thought!

We know that these lines will cost us heavily. Every time we write an exposé of this kind and try with an honest conscience before God to be faithful shepherds to those who look to us for spiritual help, there are always the incensed souls who write us all kinds of abuse and "Stop the paper" and "No more money from me!" But this is a matter far more important than money, and we have found that God is never bankrupt. Our one responsibility is to be true, the rest we leave cheerfully and confidently to Him.

A New Reformation Needed

Would that God would raise in these days of darkness a Luther or a Calvin who would storm the doors of these messengers of the Evil One, tear down their strongholds, and then raise up a standard for the true children of God to follow! The parting of the ways has come and we call upon God's children to cast out this unclean thing from them and to stand loyal to the Word of God and to refuse to support any system in the foreign fields or in the home fields which magnifies man, worships science, and dethrones the Lord Jesus Christ. Better by far to let the colleges in the Orient and the hospitals and any other institutions of learning, rot on their foundations, close their doors forever, than to continue one day longer helping to undermine faith in the Lord Jesus Christ.

And through it all we are more and more convinced that in spite of these acts of treason, God is going to turn the hearts of many, many thousands of His people toward a vigorous and unprecedented intensive gospel effort among the Jews. More and more we are seeing that in the Jew, God has wrapped up the destinies of mankind. Let us not be betrayed by those who seek to flatter the Jews, but would really damn their souls to a lost eternity. This may be God's last call to the Church of Christ to help bring about a Jewish awakening that God may use as the final means of world revival. The world is thus shaping up for the Antichrist, let us be busy while it is yet day, for the night soon will come when it will be too late.

We have felt so keenly the importance of the crisis we

have been describing to you, that we are printing this Editorial in place of the usual article we have been in the habit of writing each January, on the subject of, "To the Jew first." After all, can anything form a more powerful appeal to give the Gospel to the Jew first, than the facts we have produced here with their inescapable indictments? How long will the Church of Christ continue to disobey His command with regard to the Gospel program? To you dear friends to whom has been given the revelation of God for these closing days of the age, may we again bring the message of other years, that once more you begin the New Year in God's way the first gift in the first month of the year, literally "To the Jew first." Again will come to you a renewed experience of His blessing and approval.

"THE TIME OF THE PROMISE"

January, 1934

A new year faces us. What it will bring forth, no human tongue can tell. The world fairly bristles with gigantic possibilities. If before the coming year is gone, the blessed Trump of God, for which we all wait so eagerly, shall have sounded, what joy will it bring to thousands of His faithful and sometimes hard pressed little ones! Perhaps with peculiar timeliness should we take to heart the loving and wise injunction of Psalm 90:12, "So teach us to number our days, that we may apply our hearts unto wisdom."

A striking and thought provoking statement in Acts 7:17 caused us considerable pause recently as we were reading that touching confession and apologetic of young Stephen, the first Jewish martyr for the Lord Jesus Christ. And the more we pondered over the pregnant words, the more we realized their value to us in the present day and hour, as a guide to the learning of how to "number our days." The verse reads,

"But when the time of the promise drew nigh, which God had sworn to Abraham, the people grew and multiplied in Egypt." Acts 7:17.

The Israelites were weak and few in number when they went down to settle and establish a home in Egypt. And they continued few in number, and rather insignificant. Then suddenly, as "the time of the promise drew nigh," Israel began to multiply and grow, until the whole land of Egypt was filled with Abraham's seed. And the most authentic history tells us that the Israelites came out of Egypt some two million strong—perhaps more! Not a bad showing from a start of

Jacob's twelve sons some two hundred and thirty years before!

The Modern Parallel

The point is, that this miraculous phenomenon happened only when "the time of the promise drew nigh." And it was followed by persecution, affliction, and a definite program of extermination by means of Pharaoh's resort to infanticide, so that by the slaughter of the new-born babies it would only be a matter of time when there would be no more Israelites. Such was the devil's plan to thwart God's program for Israel.

And now let us look at the modern world for a moment, and we may be surprised to see a remarkable parallel. Not so many hundreds of years ago, in the middle ages, before America was discovered, there were in the whole world less than one million Jews. It was in that century that the Jewish race came nearest to total extinction in all of these nineteen hundred years of the Christian Era. But in the year 1800 the total had jumped to three million Jews. Then followed a century of such merciless Jew hate and massacre and burning and drowning that no race could humanly ever have survived, but would have been totally destroyed. But, contrary to human experience, the year 1900, a century later, found in the world some twelve million Jews! They had quadrupled in one hundred years of violent world hatred and bloodshed. And, wonderful as it may seem, the beginning of the present year finds in the world nearly sixteen million Jews! They have increased $33\frac{1}{3}\%$ in thirty years' time, and again in the face of persecution and suppression. Certainly, no other race or nation, even under the most favorable solidarity and privilege can show such a record. Is there not food for thought here to the child of God seeking to understand and know "the time of the promise"?

God's Purpose

Now of course God has a purpose in such a carefully worked out development. For there is no haphazard with God. And this purpose with regard to Israel is twofold, as so many of God's prophetic symbols are. First, we may mention the testing of the Gentile nations as such. The frightful punishment of the goat-nations in Matthew 24 is to be on the basis of "What have you done to my scattered people of Israel?" And conversely, the reward to the sheep-nations of the same chapter is to be on the basis of having done a kindness unto the "least of these, my brethren." And so God scatters the Jews under every sun, and among all nations, that in the last day these Jewish victims of world hate shall rise in condemnation against those Gentile nations, who will then be without excuse.

Debauching The Jews

Rather shameful are the facts of history as they reveal relentlessly how that these Gentile nations have always debauched and demoralized the Jews who had come as strangers to dwell among them. Under the title of "Brilliant and Brutal Impurity," the Sunday School Times in its issue of December 2, 1933, tells of the vile corruption and unspeakable immoralities which prevailed among the Romans in their heyday of splendor. So much so that Paul had to turn away in utter and nauseating disgust, and say, "It is a shame even to speak of those things which are done of them in secret." And this is a fair sample of the moral corruption among Gentile nations, into which the Jews found themselves plunged over and over again, throughout these nineteen hundred years of civilization. It is a miracle that there is any purity of moral standards left to the Jewish race, and the miracle becomes intensified when we learn that even today the Jews as a people still hold reputation for maintaining the highest moral and ethical standards of any people on the face of the earth! What a testimony to God's covenant-keeping faithfulness! Here in America, if we take only one example as an illustration, it will help us to understand more clearly. Let us take the American educational system, the Universities, the Colleges, and even down to the High Schools. And what do we find? How well do we personally remember, in our younger days in college, the gross immoralities, the disgusting vileness, from which the Lord in His mercy spared us. And from reports that are everywhere extant, the present day educational institutions are permeated with such teaching of moral looseness that we are brought back once more to the "black paganism of Paul's day."

And in all this, the Jew is only a minority guest. And if the modern day is turning out a generation of young Jews who have wandered far from the moorings of the fathers, will not God hold these Gentile nations to account for such debauchery? There are Gentile professors who teach godlessness and free love. It is Gentile authors like Bertrand Russel, Havelock Ellis, H. G. Wells, Judge Lindsay, and Bernard Shaw, who are seeking to destroy world faith in God, and establish a "religion" of vile paganism.

The Test Of The Church

Then, the second purpose of God with regard to Jewish dispersion is to test the Church. To the Church He gave the divine commission, "To the Jew First." And it shall ever be to her shame and confusion that she has wilfully set aside God's solemn command, just as though a Holy God never had even mentioned it, and has proceeded entirely on her own notion, on an uncharted sea of world conquest! The big nations! That's the idea! What care we for a handful of miserable Jews? And so they embarked on a program of "Christ-ianizing the world" with utter disregard of God's clearly defined plan and order. And what is the result? The heathen have heathenized the Church! And we have the astounding spectacle of a Rockefeller financed Committee of "Appraisal" telling the world that we must fuse the peerless Gospel of the Lord Jesus Christ with the filthy and unspeakably vile "re-ligions" of those about whom Paul said, "It is a shame even to speak of those things." Ephesians 5 : 12.

A Primary Responsibility

In a recent issue of The Presbyterian, that remarkable layman, Hugh R. Monro, who, though engaged in a multi-plicity of business activities which would tax the energies of most men, still makes it his business to devote an astonishing amount of his time and talent for the cause of the Gospel of the Lord Jesus Christ, writes an article entitled "The Retribu-tion of Neglect" in which he shows how the Church of Christ is being punished of God today because of her sins of omis-sion throughout the centuries. One arresting paragraph is this:

"The Church has failed to recognize its debt to Israel and the evangelization of the Jew as a primary responsibility. Result: The alienation from the Church of God's ancient people, and their calamitous drift into spiritual indifference and infidelity."

This is simply another way of bringing home to the Lord's people the fundamental fact of the Gospel revelation, that the Church must plan its worldwide missionary program on the one doctrinal platform, "To the Jew first." And, to have a layman of the spiritual insight and church standing of Dr. Hugh R. Monro, call the attention of the Church to this failing, is a rebuke that cannot go unheeded. It is also an evidence that the Lord is working today; when the church leaders themselves fail to do God's will, then God begins to speak to the followers.

Disappointing Results

And it may come with surprise to many, as it certainly did to us, when we read not so long ago, the official statistics released in The Literary Digest, as to actual numbers of Christians in Japan and China. In Japan, for instance, after seventy years of the Church's program to "conquer Japan" the total number of Christians, that is, names on books, is 224,000. This, out of a population of 90,000,000, which means one-quarter of one per cent of the population! In China, the showing is even poorer, for they show 446,000 out of a population of 440,000,000, or about one-tenth of one per cent of the present population! And this, after nearly one hundred years of intensive work, with millions of dollars spent; spent for universities to teach American "science" and "higher criticism"; millions spent for hospitals, millions for missionaries, and for stations. And God forbid that we should say a word in detraction of Foreign Missions. The Church certainly has done too little, in this direction, shamefully so. We are only mentioning the facts as to results, so as to afford a basis for comparison with what could be accomplished if we did things God's way.

It Really Works

And now, turn a moment to Jewish conversions. No blare of trumpets, no beating of drums, no five year programs, no Interchurch World movement—nothing. No organization to build up a machine for Jewish missionary undertakings. No colleges for Jewish Christians, the nearest we have is the Jewish Missions Course of the Moody Bible

Institute of Chicago, and what a hard time even that department has to get its support! No hospitals for Jewish Christians, no endowments, no seminaries! And yet in the face of all that shameful showing, here are just two or three astonishing facts, to show that God's order "To the Jew First" really works, and that the Lord knew what He was talking about when He commanded us to begin at Jerusalem.

First, take America. It is of course difficult to secure accurate figures here, because the Jews, when they accept the Lord Jesus Christ, become lost in the Churches, and their interests and their means go into the channels of the Churches they have joined. But there are several fairly dependable estimates, and they vary from 25,000 to 50,000. Let us take the smaller figure, that is, 25,000 Jewish Christians in America. Now there are in America 4,000,000 Jews. And so 25,000 converts would mean five-eighths of one per cent, or two and one-half times the ratio of Japan, and over six times the ratio of China!

What a rebuke this is from God! And think how many more Jewish believers there would be if the Church should be awakened out of her ignorance and indifference! Christian Science alone claims 75,000 Jews in America! Think of that tragedy! For it shows that the Jew is approachable and is hungry for new light, since he has lost faith in his own Judaism through his contact with our American schools and civilization.

But Germany affords us more accurate and still more astonishing figures. For the Hitler enactments of Jew hate have crystallized and brought to the surface facts which no one ever knew existed. By ordering all Jews out of the churches, and all those who had the slightest trace of Jewish blood through intermarriage for several generations past, the amazing fact was revealed that over 200,000 members of Christian

Churches in Germany were of Jewish extraction! Of these, more than 60,000 were full blooded Jews, converts of the present generation!

Now the total Jewish population of Germany is 560,000 Jews. So we have 60,000, or better than ten per cent full blooded Jews who have been found to be believers! This compares with one-tenth of one per cent for China, and one-quarter of one per cent for Japan!

"To The Jew First"

Do you not see how God stands ready to bless the Church if she but follow His Command "To the Jew first"? If, with so little done for Israel, God has blest so wonderfully, how much more will He bless if we really do His bidding in earnest? Is it not drawing very near to "the time of the promise"? And has not God put the Jew at our door, to test the Church? And shall we fail at the testing? And may it not be that He will use us if we are yielded to His will for Israel, to prepare those 144,000 Jews for the tribulation days so that through their testimony many thousands of your Gentile relatives may be saved, and form that "great multitude, which no man could number, of all nations" who will join in that shout of ecstasy, and cry out, "Salvation to our God which sitteth upon the Throne, and unto the Lamb"? You see, a vote for Jewish missions is a vote for ultimate Gentile conversion!

The Invitation

So, dear friends, we close by asking, Are you ready and willing to obey God for this year by solemnly undertaking to do God's work in God's way, "To the Jew First"? "Come thou with us, and we will do thee good," in the name of the Lord Jesus Christ.

What say you?

JEW HATE RAMPANT

January, 1935

If it is proper to wish you a Happy New Year, we do so heartily and eagerly. And since every turning of the wheel of time brings us that much nearer to that long looked for hour when He shall come, and "shall not tarry," we may with the earnest good wish, pass on to you the precious prayer of Psalm 90:12, "so teach us to number our days, that we may cause our hearts to arrive at wisdom." (Literal Hebrew).

But is it not strange that in neither the present-day Jewish calendar nor in the calendar used by the Gentile world, is God's sacred order of the months heeded? Exodus 12:2 gives clearly the sequence of the sacred calendar, for here God told the Israelites, "This month (Nisan) shall be unto you the beginning of months; it shall be the first month of the year to you." Nisan corresponds closely to April in our present calendar, which is the season of spring, when the rains come, and the ground is fertile and the grass is green and all nature begins to awake and take on new life. How fitting that it should be the beginning, the head month of the year. And it is also the time when Israel was delivered from the Egyptian yoke, and so how doubly fitting that Israel starts out, a free man, ransomed by God, on the first month, the beginning of a new year!

All Have Sinned

But just as Paul shows in Romans that the whole human race has sinned before God, the Jew with the law and the Gentile without the law; so here again is evidence that the Jew, having been given God's calendar of the months, has ignored the order, and established an order of his own; while

the Gentile never even took the trouble to ascertain whether
God had a calendar, but went to his own heathen mythology
and made up his calendar. So, once more, human character,
both Jew and Gentile, fails under the test. And no Jew can
tell you why he keeps Tishri, the seventh month, for his New
Year! He only knows he does it, by order of the rabbis.

But to the born-again child of God, every day starts a new
year, and we know not of times or seasons, of feasts or holy
days. Every day we start afresh with Him, Who alone commands the morning, Who alone knows the ordinances of
heaven; and we have the blessed assurance that "the Lord's
mercies. . .are new every morning." Lamentations 3:23. And
well is it for us that often in the midst of sorrow and despair,
when the very space around us seems to turn black, we suddenly become aware of His presence, and we rejoice with the
poet who wrote:

> "Sometimes a light surprises
>   The Christian while he sings:
> It is the Lord who rises,
>   With healing in His wings.
> When comforts are declining,
>   He grants the soul, again,
> A season of clear shining,
>   To cheer it after rain."

We have digressed far from what we began to write.
Yet we feel perhaps God had a purpose in the digression.

Our pages are again crammed with the accounts of the
marvelous doings of our Lord in our midst. We seem never
to have room enough to tell all that our friends are so eager
to know. We ask that you will forgive us the taking of valuable space for the symposium on the stupid invention known
as the Protocols, on another page. We do it only because

many friends are still puzzled over this demoniacal instrument of Jew-hate; and we have rejoiced on former occasions to know that our vigorous exposure of the sham and hypocrisy of those engaged in this shameful business has been the means of saving many from the snares and delusions of the Evil One. So, do forgive us just this once more, and help us put it in the hands of those to whom it will come as a revelation and a blessing. It was with sadness of heart that we read a few days ago the following paragraph in the annual report issued by the Moody Bible Institute of Chicago, through Dr. James M. Gray:

"We regret that no such encouraging report can be made of our Jewish Missions Course, the Director of which believes that anti-Semitic propaganda has assumed such alarming proportions as to have dried up the source of support for this work on behalf of the Jews. Jewish mission stations have been closed and their forces reduced, with the result that there is a lessened incentive for young people to train for Jewish mission work. However, we are hopeful that conditions may improve in the near future."

Does one need stronger proof that the so-called Protocol propaganda is of the devil?

Result Of Disobedience

And it is noteworthy that among those "Fundamentalists" and "Bible Teachers" who have been the most busy in their campaigns of Jew-hate, are to be found the very men who have deliberately disobeyed God's solemnly given order in missions, "To the Jew First!" So we must expect quite naturally that such a one, having turned a deaf ear to God's command, and substituted his own foolish "interpretation" of God's clearly worded teaching, should find himself in darker and ever darker ramblings of satanic delusions, until as has been the case with one such "teacher" some one remarked, "He is beside himself." We thank God that He has kept you all faithful to this testimony, and that you have resisted boldly the assaults of these unconscious servants of the devil's plans. This is all that has kept your Mission alive, and saved it from such a tragic story as the one quoted above.

Near The End?

It was toward the end of Israel's career in Palestine that her leaders became blinded, and their hearts hardened. And the reason simmered down to this, that they had gradually and finally refused to witness to the Gentiles! This was the thing God had called them out to do, to be a light to the Gentiles. Just to think, God had picked out this handful of Israelites, a sort of Gideon's army, and had committed unto them the oracles of God, that they might bring the whole world to the knowledge of the true God. But the reformed rabbi today loves to denounce these "terrible Jewish missionaries—apostates," because they "steal Jewish souls." And then the rabbi adds, with self-righteous pride, "but we Jews are a non-proselyting people; we believe that if you are born a Jew you must die a Jew and if you are born a Christian you must die a Christian." Poor, deluded rabbi! He may not know it, but every time he makes a statement of this sort he is advertising to the world that he and all Jews who follow his example, are an apostate and disobedient people, violating and nullifying the very *primum mobile* of their existence!

And so it came to pass that Israel made a fatal mistake: instead of using the commission which God had given them that they become a light to the Gentiles, as a great obligation that must rest on their shoulders and that should serve only to humble them, such as the apostle Paul declared, with the same sense of humbled obligation, "I am debtor both to the Greeks and to the barbarians, both to the wise and the unwise." Instead of this attitude, Israel took these obligations as a means for personal aggrandizement, to be made only to cater to her pride and conceit. So that Israel actually built about herself a wall of exclusion, and virtually said to the Gentile world, "We are holier than you, to us God gave the commands, to you He gave none; we will have nothing to do with you, we will not even eat with you, we consider you as unworthy to associate with us." All of this, in spite of the fact that there was ever present the daily reminder in the silent, but eloquent testimony of the Court of the Gentiles, which formed a permanent part of the Temple grounds themselves.

The Tables Turned

The Holy Word tells us, "Through their fall salvation is come unto the Gentiles, for to provoke them (the Jews) to jealousy." Romans 11:11. And here we have a statement worthy of the closest scrutiny of every child of God in these days of confusion. The Lord practically said to Israel, "Very well, I have given you a chance for two thousand years to give my testimony to the Gentiles, and now you have failed, and so I am going to do a new thing in the world; I am going to turn to the Gentiles and give them a chance to hear the Gospel, and I am going to test them out just as I have tested you out: as I told you to be my witnesses to the Gentiles, now I shall tell the Gentiles to be my witnesses to you Jews." And this is exactly what happened and here we have it clearly stated, that the purpose of God in calling out from among the Gentiles an ecclesia for His name, is that through these Gentiles the testimony of the Gospel shall be given to the Jew, thus provoking the Jew to jealousy and bringing him back once more to God through the Lord Jesus Christ.

Human Nature Always The Same

But what do we behold in the present hour? Do the
Gentiles go to the Jews with the Gospel? Have not the Gentiles failed in their obligation to the Jew just as miserably
as the Jews failed in their obligation to the Gentiles? Here
we have a nineteen hundred year swing of the pendulum
during which time the Gentiles have had complete domination of the Church and her destinies. What have the Gentiles
done with that responsibility? And suppose that the Lord
Jesus Christ were to come to earth today as He came two
thousand years ago, how many churches would actually receive Him as a Jew? And how many Jews would He find
that the Church had brought into His body? The Bishop of
Worcester recently delivered a really startling address in
London on the Church and the Jews. We wish we had space
for the whole address, but one or two paragraphs only can
find their way into these columns, and these I have selected
just to show how that man of God has been completely
humiliated with the sense of the Church's failure to obey the
teaching of the Word of God. Here are the paragraphs:

"It was not until Christianity in the time of Constantine
became first a tolerated and then the dominant religion of the
Empire that there began that terrible era, which has lasted
to our time, wherein the Church by its deliberate choice
and conduct, has made itself one gigantic and seemingly
impenetrable obstacle between the Jews and the figure of Our
Blessed Lord.

"If the Church today is to make reparation for the past;
if we are ever to see the fulfillment of the Apostle's startling
words, 'If the casting away of them be the reconciling of the
world, what shall the receiving of them be, but life from the
dead?'—what, then, must we do? We must study history.
Few Christians know anything of Jewish history subsequent

to the New Testament. They do not dream of the chasm of misconception and prejudice that separate the Jews from Christians, of the bitter memories of racial and personal wrongs, and of the attitude of unyielding opposition to Christ and Christianity which has become an integral part of Jewish tradition. Knowledge will bring not merely an overwhelming sense of shame, and a lively desire for reparation, but also a new sympathy and understanding which will enable us to make the approach with humility and tactfulness.

"We must more deeply consider the strategic importance of the Jew in the missionary enterprise. Anyone who will think of the commanding influence of the Jew in all the nations, and not least in our own, will realize the potential force for the furtherance of the Kingdom of a people, virile, gifted, and persistent."

There Is Always A Faithful Remnant

And this only shows that just as God had among ancient Israel the faithful remnant, the Nathaniels without guile, the Simeons waiting in the Temple for the "consolation of Israel," so in these corresponding days of twilight and darkness, He does have, in the professing Church, that true Ecclesia, the "inner circle" who likewise in all simplicity and dead earnestness, hold fast to the promises of God, and seek to do His revealed will as being the only worth-while objective in all the world. It was a rare privilege, and we were strangely moved, a few days ago, to have received from a devoted and self-sacrificing servant of God, and a beloved friend of the Mission, a copy of a letter he had sent to the pastor of his boyhood church; it was on the occasion of his mother's home-going, and the pastor had conducted the funeral services, and our friend sent him this beautiful letter of appreciation, revealing a heart full of love and devotion to a saintly soul that now waits for him on the other shore. And in that letter, he took special occasion to explain his love for the Jewish Mission testimony, an explanation which may well be a classic apologetic for every lover of Israel. We pass on to you a few paragraphs:

"The command I hear is for the salvation of His brethren after the flesh through the American Board of Missions to the Jews. Though a far cry from the appeals in my boyhood for the heathen in Africa, China and India, still the example of Mother's faith and the influence of the earlier congregation of your church may have thus been instrumental through God during the last twenty years, in adding to His crown Jewish jewels which I cannot help but feel may be nearest to His heart.

"It is our hope and prayer, just as it was the hope of Jewish women for centuries to give birth to the Messiah, that in saving Jewish souls we may be used to save that last necessary Jewish soul to complete His body and Bride and thus hasten His coming from the right hand of God to complete our redemption.

"Further do we desire to leave our corporation, when we are caught up by supernatural powers beyond our own, as a ready implement for use by that Godly Jewish remnant, who, awakened by the Rapture, shall preach the Gospel of the Kingdom unto all nations. And possibly by this use of our headquarters and branches our country may be reckoned with the sheep nations when Jesus comes with us to judge the nations according to their reception of this Godly remnant during the seven years of their ministry from the Rapture to Mount Olivet.

"With this in our hearts we leave the Jew otherwise to the judgment of God for guilt, being instructed not to judge before the time for us to judge the earth, and, who are we

to judge inasmuch as the Jews delivered up our Creator to us
to scourge and crucify?"

Irrevocably Ordained

Now we have said enough, but all of it only to show our
dear friends once more and this time from a slightly different angle, the renewed importance of that which we have
taught for these many years, that the Gospel still must be
given, as God has ordained it irrevocably, "to the Jew first."
Certainly a sense of shame because of the wrongs done this
people for nineteen hundred years should, aside from all
other valid Scripture arguments, cause us to hasten to bring
the balm of the Gospel of the Lord Jesus Christ, just as He
commanded us, "To the Jew first."

So once more, as we have done these many years before,
in this first month of what the world calls its new year, we
invite you every one to begin as so many already have formed
the blessed practice of doing, with the first gift of the year
literally to the Jew first. We do believe that because we have
steadfastly built this Mission upon that one foundation rock
of Scripture, and have refused to be downed or ridiculed, or
talked out of it, the Lord has honored and blessed this Mission, so that in this tragic hour it is one of the most important
and most potent factors in God's hands for the promulgation
of the Gospel among the Jews throughout the earth. And He
has given to us a wonderfully blessed fellowship with the
many dear friends who have been holding up our hands in
this testimony, for which we wish once more to record our
everlasting gratitude to our Heavenly Father, as indeed we
have done many, many times before.

The Lord has spoken good concerning Israel, and that
good will like a contagion spread to all who take part with
God in helping to bring to fruition His purposes in that
nation, and through that nation in the whole world.

CONTRARY TO NATURE

January, 1936

Janus was an ancient Italian idol. The Romans called him the god of beginnings; he had two faces, one looking east and one looking west. From this heathen divinity we got the name January for the first month of our Julian calendar. The theory was that just as the god Janus looked both ways, so the month January looks over the year that has passed, and looks forward to the year that is to come.

There comes a time when it is good to stop for a moment by way of reflection, and to consider the days that have gone, and the days that are to come. The one, in retrospect; the other, in prospect. But the child of God does not need heathen idolatries to cause him to indulge in these necessary retrospections, for the Lord has Himself given us abundant authority and incentive to do this. What can be more beautiful than the majestic stateliness of the cadences of the 90th Psalm? And what can be more impressive as a climax to the poignant and divine philosophies of these sacred words, than the 12th verse:

> To number our days—thus teach us,
> That we may win ourselves a heart of wisdom.

We have put down the free translation from the Hebrew. The Hebrew word translated in the authorized version "that we may apply our hearts unto wisdom," Dr. Delitzsch pointed out, is the word used in connection with agriculture, and means, to bear away, to carry off, to gain, properly to bring in, as one might bring into the barn the produce of the field. Thus the prayer of the Psalmist takes on rare beauty and strength. We are to remember our days, realizing how fleeting they are, and we are to lay to heart the solemn truth that God's wrath is irrevocably set against sin; and then as a result of such meditation and prayer we shall bring home, as from a ripened harvest field, the choicest fruit which life can yield—a heart of wisdom. Thus, in the words of that sainted scholar, Alexander Maclaren, the heart "having learned the power of God's anger, and the number of our days, turns itself to the eternal dwelling place, and no more is sad when it sees life ebbing away or the generations moving in unbroken succession into the darkness." Here then is true Christian philosophy, and here is the anchor which will hold the child of God steady in these days of shifting sands and unstable foundations.

True Wisdom

There is moreover a progressive wisdom that is vouchsafed to the child of God. The first step of true wisdom is of course to know God, and to enter into relationship with Him as His child. The next step is to be taught of Him through the ever-abiding ministry of the Holy Spirit. The promise is "If ye continue in my word, then are ye my disciples indeed; and ye shall know the truth, and the truth shall make you free." John 8:31-32. And because we, who are directly engaged in the divinely committed task of giving the Jew the Gospel message, are especially interested in knowing His Truth, we are ever seeking to discover the place which God has given the Jew in His program for the Church. So we come directly to the question, and we hope we shall be able to show that this is indeed the heart of all questions, "How much wisdom has the Church brought to her own heart by way of seeking to learn whether God has special instructions as to the method He would have the Church use in her world wide missionary program?" For nearly fifty years this mission has staked everything upon what we have been pro-

foundly convinced must be the fundamental premise upon
which the missionary work of the church is to be carried
on—"To the Jew First." And each first month of the year
we have asked the Lord to give us some little message containing perhaps a new angle of light from which one of the
facets of this diamond of God's truth could be viewed, and
perhaps a new and richer sparkle of color and illumination
might be revealed. And somehow the Lord has always
answered these prayers, and has given us a fresh illumination
of His Holy Word; and it has been a blessed privilege to
receive from many of our friends their words of gratitude
because of the new light given; and we many times praise
Him for this privilege.

Contrary To Nature

We were struck with peculiar force as we restudied recently the teaching of Romans 11:24:

"For if thou wert cut out of, the olive tree which is wild
by nature, and wert graffed contrary to nature into a good
olive tree; how much more shall these, which be the natural
branches, be graffed into their own olive tree?"

Our thought was focussed upon the expression "contrary
to nature" and we have pondered much over this striking
phrase. In the 17th verse of this chapter the apostle Paul
tells us that the Gentile believers in Rome were as the wild
olive tree, grafted in among the Jewish branches, and that
they have become partakers of the root and fatness of the
olive tree. It does not say monopolizers, nor usurpers, but it
does say partakers. But, it is a sad fact to relate that many
Gentiles have totally disregarded this fundamental doctrine,
and have been teaching that the Jews have been altogether
cast off, and that they themselves have taken the place of the
Jews in God's eternal purposes. Some have even called them-

selves spiritual Israelites, and have actually spoken of the Church as the Gentile Church; they have gone so far, in some cases, as to teach that the Jews must not be evangelized in the present day. One Bible teacher stated in our presence once that Jewish Christians must not occupy places of leadership in the present Church age!

We wonder if this colossal blunder has not meant the undoing of the Church, and if it may not be true that right at this point we may discover the parting of the ways. John Wilkinson, of London, in writing on this subject, made the following comment:

"These wild olive grafts, the Gentiles, have misunderstood their relationship to the Jewish natural branches, and to the Jewish olive tree, as partakers only with believing Jews of the root of fatness. The Gentile wild olive graft should have lost its wildness by incorporation in the Jewish Christian church as a partaker only of its blessings; but it has claimed to be a spiritual Israel, the Gentile church, and has thus produced a Gentile Christendom almost as corrupt as heathendom. The Gentile wild olive graft has subdued the good olive; it has worked according to nature instead of under the controlling and subduing influence of grace."

What an indictment, and what a solemn thing to meditate upon! For here we find ourselves stumbling full bodied upon an astounding revelation, a revelation that will be difficult for us to explain fully with our limited language and our limited space; but we shall try as best we can, and trust that the Lord through the Holy Spirit will give us the right words.

What we mean is that we shall take the statement of the 17th verse, as to the wild olive tree, and, combining it with the statement of the 24th verse, "Contrary to nature," follow through to the logical implications. Some have thought that

Paul blundered when he spoke about grafting the wild olive tree into the good branches, for grafting of olive trees is never done that way. It is the good olive branch that is grafted into the wild tree, and it is the good branch which overcomes or subdues the wild tree, and causes the wild tree to change its fruitage into good fruit. But, those who have accused Paul of making this blunder, have only revealed their own ignorance and superficiality, for if these critics had only had the foresight to read to the 24th verse, they would have discovered that Paul knew perfectly well what he was writing about, for he says in the 24th verse that this grafting mentioned in the 17th verse was done *contrary to nature*. So once again the Word of God is vindicated and its traducers confounded.

But, the real revelation comes when we travel still farther down the path now blazed for us by this new statement, "Contrary to nature." Here is the inescapable and bold logic of this teaching: When the horticulturist followed the normal and natural processes of grafting the good olive branch into the wild olive tree, the result was that the wild olive tree in due season produced edible fruit. Now let us reverse the process, and let us graft a wild branch upon a good tree, and what shall we logically expect as a sequence? Is it not correct to conclude that just exactly the reverse process will take place, that is, the wild olive branch will overcome and subdue the good tree with the ultimate result that the fruit will become wild?

The Proof Of The Pudding

Now let us observe if the theory has actually worked out in practice. What do we find? To the sorrow of all, we find the Church in a state of discouraging apostasy! After two thousand years of Gospel proclamation, the Word of God

is actually denied and blasphemed in places where it ought
to be honored and worshipped. Let us take just two or three
illustrations, to show how Christendom has become paganized
and how the wild olive branches have actually saturated the
life of the Church of Christ. Suppose we examine the calendar by which we count our days and years. Who gave us
the names of our months, such as January, February, March,
etc.? Are they taken from the Word of God? No, they are
taken from heathen mythology. Or, take the names of the
days of the week, Monday, Tuesday, Wednesday, etc. Where
do we get them? From the Bible? No, but once more from
heathen mythology. Monday is the day of the moon, Tuesday
is named after Tiw, Norse god of war, Wednesday is the
day of the old heathen god Wodin, Thursday from the god
Thor, etc. Is that Christian? Or has the wild olive branch
injected itself into our so called Christian civilization?

Or, let us take some of our holy festival days. What about
Christmas? This is the time when we are supposed to cele-
brate with holy joy the blessed birth of the Lord Jesus Christ
in Bethlehem. And of course one would expect that such an
event would command respect and worship. But what do we
do? We chop down trees! See the exact picture of ourselves
in Jere. 10:2-4:

"Thus saith the Lord, Learn not the way of heathen. For
the customs of the people are vain: for one cutteth a tree out
of the forest, the work of the hand of the workman, with
the axe. They deck it with silver and with gold: they fasten
it with nails and with hammers, that it move not."

What is this but Romanized paganism? And what else do we
hear? We hear about Santa Claus and St. Nicholas and jingle
bells! And St. Nicholas comes out of the mist of the legends
of the Norse fantasies. And here we find ourselves in the

twentieth century, with nineteen hundred years of Gospel light, chopping down trees for a mythical Santa Claus!

Then let us go a bit farther: There comes a time in the year which we call Easter, although such a name as Easter is unknown in the Word of God. The word does appear once, and that in Acts 12:14, but it is an error of the King James version, for the manuscript says Pascha, meaning Passover, not Easter. Easter is the name of a heathen festival that has no connection with the Jewish passover or with the memorial of the Lord's resurrection.

We Dye Eggs

But passing aside the name itself, let us go to the celebration. This is the time when we commemorate that most holy and important of all events, the resurrection of the Lord Jesus Christ from the dead. What do we do? We roll colored eggs on the White House lawn! We buy bunny rabbits! We buy chocolate hens sitting on candy eggs! And as for the church services, are they not more often a display of the newest fashions in clothing rather than a sincere worship of the heart? Is it not rather a sinister thing that New York must have its Fifth Avenue Easter parade year after year, and so Chicago, and so London, and so throughout the world?

Is it not after all the startling evidence that the wild olive tree has overcome the good? And has not Christendom become paganized? This paganizing has extended itself into the very heart of the church ritual. Imagine our astonishment when we picked up a newspaper not long ago, and read the following item:

"While the minister and a capacity Sunday crowd looked on, Ruth St. Denis danced a 'rhythmic interpretation of the Psalms' before the altar of the Park Avenue Presbyterian church. The dancer went through motions that she said symbolized 'the gradual ascent of man's soul from the moment he acknowledges his need of spiritual light to the final radiation.' Barefooted and clad in a long, simple black robe with flowing sleeves, Miss St. Denis pantomimed tragedy and despair before a gilt throne set atop a modernistic arrangement of gold blocks. With dancing movements she led the church members through the hymn 'Come, Thou Almighty King.' White of hair and pale of face, the only color she displayed was the carmine of her lips, fingernails and toenails. A 'first reader' and a 'second reader,' one in the pulpit, read passages from the Psalms and from Miss St. Denis' writings amplifying them. Rev. Edmund M. Wylie introduced Miss St. Denis."

Just think, a theatrical dancer appearing in the pulpit of the Presbyterian Church on a Sunday morning in the city of New York! And here is the sickening irony of such a situation: So far as we have been able to discover, there was no protest made on the part of the New York Presbytery, nor were there charges brought against this church or against the pastor for conduct unbecoming the Presbyterian Church. But, and this is what is alarmingly ominous, let a Dr. Machen, filled with a sense of outrage because of disloyalty to the Word of God on the part of certain missionaries under the Presbyterian Foreign Mission Board, finally break out in righteous protest that these conditions ought not to be, and what happens? They would hang him! He is called a traitor, and he is excommunicated! How sadly has Satan blinded us!

And now, does it not become more and more clear that there was divine wisdom in the instructions given to the Church that she should take the Gospel "To the Jew first"? What unusual blessings the Church must have forfeited in having failed to carry out this primary obligation. Is it not reasonable to suppose that if the Church had kept within her borders the Jewish Christian testimony, the bloodless religion of today would be an impossibility? Because the Jew of all peoples has been brought up to know what blood sacrifice means. Do you suppose that if in some of these so-called Modernistic churches there were even a dozen Jewish Christians as members, do you suppose that the sacrilegious mouthings of the Modernistic preachers of those churches could long continue? Just see how the church made the fatal blunder of keeping the Jews out of her membership, and now see what has been the result. Here is a terrible indictment which we quote from a recently published letter written by the Bishop of Worcester:

"It was not until Christianity in the time of Constantine became first a tolerated and then the dominant religion of the Empire that there began that terrible era, which has lasted to our own time, wherein the church, by its deliberate choice and conduct, has made itself one gigantic and seemingly impenetrable obstacle between the Jews and the figure of Our Blessed Lord.

"Probably to the better treatment of the Jews in Europe and America during the first quarter of this century is due the fact that after generations of innumerable Jews had come and gone without pronouncing the name of Jesus, there was actually published in 1922 in Jerusalem, and by the foremost orthodox Jewish scholar of our time, Dr. Klausner's 'Jesus of Nazareth.' Dr. Wise, an American Liberal Jew, defending the publication of that book, significantly asks the question: 'Shall Jews forever refuse to claim Jesus either because of the centuries of misunderstanding and Christlessness which have grown out of the stories touching the manner of his death, or because Christendom is not yet become Christian'?

"Recent happenings, alas! are once more veiling the face of Our Lord from His own race. A new wave of anti-Semitism is affecting many countries all over the world. In Roumania a Prime Minister has been murdered by the agent of an anti-Jewish organization on whose activities he had put checks. In Germany, not only has the Government excluded from all State office all Jews, and even those who have but one Jewish grand-parent, but a large party in the German Evangelical Church actually secured church legislation applying the same rule to all pastors and other holders of office in the Prussian church and some other regional churches. There are, moreover, disquieting signs that anti-Semitic feeling, partly roused by the influx of large numbers of Jewish refugees from Germany, is on the increase in our own land.

"We must more deeply consider the strategic importance of the Jew in the missionary enterprise. Anyone who will think of the commanding influence of the Jew in all the nations, and not least in our own, will realize the potential force for the furtherance of the Kingdom of a people, virile, gifted, and persistent."

And now this letter has assumed lengths we had no idea would be the case when we started out, but here it is, and may God bless it to the enlightenment of unprejudiced souls seeking His truth.

Come Thou With Us

For a good many years now we have opened the Lord's treasury at this time, the first month of the calendar year, and invited our many dear and faithful friends to make their offerings for the Lord's work literally "To the Jew first." And somehow the Lord has honored this practice, and year after year has seen always an increasing host of His devoted people adopting this divine method. And if only we had space to print the testimonies of blessings that have come into the lives of these dear ones! And how many letters of thanks have come to us, and how our hearts have been gladdened because our faithfulness to this fundamental truth, has been thus honored and blessed of God.

So, once more, we open the flood gates and say to our beloved friends, "Come thou with us and we will do thee good; for the Lord has spoken good concerning Israel." The outpouring of the gifts of January always means that we have a first class start for the budget of the new year, and of course our friends know that we make every dollar do one hundred cents' worth of Gospel testimony. This past year you have enabled us to stretch our lines throughout the earth as we have never done before. May the coming year prove likewise a record breaking year not only in gifts and prayers for the Jewish work, but also in what He will allow us to accomplish for His honor and glory throughout the months to come. Perhaps there are not very many months left, but whether they be few or many, God grant that we shall be found faithful to the trust He has committed to us, "To the Jew first."

CHINA TESTIFIES, "TO THE JEW FIRST!"

January, 1937

The beginning of a new year stirs old memories. It is human to look back. What mistakes we have made! What wrongs we have done! Of what injustices have we been guilty! And how our soul is tormented with remorse and self-blame. We are moved to make new resolutions, to "turn a new page," as it were. But all this to no avail; for after a while we stumble again, and the flesh once more fails us.

The divine method is different; and it provides the remedy for the aching heart. Hear what the Holy Spirit has to teach us through Paul:

"Brethren, I count not myself to have apprehended: but this one thing I do, forgetting those things which are behind, and reaching forth unto those things which are before, I press toward the mark" (Phil. 3:13, 14).

Forgetting those things which are behind! All things of the flesh will fail. "In my flesh dwelleth no good thing," cried Paul, and ended his self-examination with the heart-breaking exclamation, "O wretched man that I am!" So the cure is to forget those things which are behind—forget the betrayal of friendship; forget wrongs done to us, and wrongs done by us; forget the losses of life, of fortune, of possessions; forget the mistakes of bad judgment; forget the aches and pains of last year. Leave them all to our Lord. For your own shortcomings, make amends as His Word prescribes. Then, having done all, commit yourself and your all to the One who "able to keep that which I have committed unto Him against that day."

For all flesh is as grass. The years come and the years go,

and they add sorrow and perplexity to our lives except as we have learned to look to God, Who alone is eternal. It is beautifully put before us in Hebrews 1:11, that even the earth and the heavens which the Lord has made shall perish: "But thou remainest; and they all shall wax old as doth a garment;... but thou art the same, and thy years shall not fail."

Brighter Than The Sun's Rays

"Thou remainest." In Psalm 72 there is a wonderful verse which explicitly sets forth the everlasting nature of the Lord Jesus Christ. It is a verse worth meditating over at this time of "New Year" thinking. We refer to v. 17, in which the English of the A. V. does not accurately convey the meaning of the original Hebrew. Literally, it reads:

"May his name be forever,
May his name put forth shoots before the sun,
And may people bless themselves in him,
May all peoples call him happy."

This Psalm presents what is perhaps the most perfect and vivid picture of the blessedness to come upon the earth in the time of the Messiah's reign. The hopes and ideals cherished for the brilliant reign of Solomon were never realized by him, but will find their most blessed fulfillment in that Greater than Solomon when He shall establish His beneficent reign upon this earth.

The strength and beauty of the verse quoted is found in the assurance it contains of God's eternity. The first word of the verse is kin to the name which God gave Moses—the *I am*. That is, He *is* forever; a creative fiat. It is the *I am* and the *I shall be*. The idea of endurance in the sense of human frailty is not there—it is the divine existence, the sovereign declaration, *I am*.

The second phrase is even more striking—"may his name put forth shoots before the sun." Another translation of this clause is also valid:

"Before the sun, Jinnon is his name."

The striking word here is Jinnon. It means, to put forth shoots, to extend oneself, to exist eternally, without end. Hence the translation, "put forth, or radiate, shoots, before the sun." According to the Talmud and the Midrash, Jinnon is one of the eight names of the Messiah; and as this is the only place in all the Bible where this word Jinnon occurs, the evidence is clear that the Jewish Rabbins themselves understood this Psalm to refer to the Messianic reign.

So the teaching is that our blessed Lord shall exist forever; that His Messianic rays of power and beauty shall shine even with the brightness of the sun, and being brighter than the sun, shall outlast them. It is the pre-statement of the truth of Hebrews 1:11, "Thou remainest."

"Thou Who Changest Not"

So this is the word of cheer for us as the new year opens. Our confidence, in the midst of the years of change and confusion, must be in Him Who changes not, but abides forever. It is the prayer of Henry F. Lyte in the beautiful hymn:

"Swift to its close ebbs out life's little day;
Earth's joys grow dim, its glories pass away;
Change and decay in all around I see;
O Thou, who changest not, abide with me!"

But we must stop. It was our intention to bring you a January exhortation, according to our annual custom, concerning your privilege and practice of these many years in the matter of world-wide missions—to the Jew first. Upon this Scriptural rock the Lord has founded your Jewish Mission, and has heaped upon it forty-two years of ever widening usefulness and blessing. We believe one reason for this remarkable testimony is that we have learned to put first things first; and with the foundation sure, the superstructure is safe. And while our friends see eye to eye with us on this fundamental doctrine in Missions, yet they somehow love to have the teaching re-emphasized from time to time, on the principle of Psalms 107:2, "Let the redeemed of the Lord say so."

This time, instead of giving new arguments, or even old ones, we have an unusual privilege—we shall give you an actual testimony. More unusual still, the testimony is from far-off China, from a dear, devoted child of God, a humble missionary at work for the Lord in Shanghai. Her name is Mrs. Zella Mussen. She has graciously given us permission to use her experience, if only it may prove a blessing to others. You may be interested to know also that from China we receive gifts regularly for the work, gifts not only from missionaries of the Cross, but gifts from the poorest of Chinese converts, who wish to obey literally the Bible command, "to the Jew first." Is it not significant that the foreign missionary sees God's order more clearly than many of us at home; and so, too, the unsophisticated convert! But here is Mrs. Mussen's testimony:

"In the latter part of 1929, after returning to China from furlough, I was talking with a Shanghai missionary concerning the blessing that had been following her work, both spiritually and temporally. She made the following comment: 'Yes, the Lord has blessed us, and I believe it is because we have for years made it a habit in our Chinese Church to give the entire offering on the first Sunday of each month toward Christian work among the Jews. Our Chinese have this vision and give liberally toward this, and frequently our offering for this particular Sunday exceeds that of others where the money is used for our own Chinese work.'

"Here was an entirely new thought to me. I had given a dollar here or there toward this purpose, and once in a while two dollars, and, at the very most, once or twice, five dollars toward work amongst the Jews, but never had the thought of systematic giving in this direction crossed my mind. The thought came, 'If this is something that so pleases the Lord, I want to adopt it also.' So then and there the resolution was made that the entire tithe of the first month of each year would be given for Christian work amongst His chosen people.

"Before returning to China I had undertaken some heavy obligations and, upon reaching Shanghai, found that exchange had become so unfavorable that one American dollar required about three of our Shanghai dollars, and payments in gold back home at the above rate gave me a vision of months of grinding out money. It loomed large on the horizon. However, the very first time I made the offering for the Gospel among the Jews—that month word came that some funds which had been tied up for years were available to me. It was some hundreds of dollars, and it very materially helped the financial burden at that time. I was duly impressed.

"The next year, January and February passed and it was not until March that the Jewish offering was sent. In May I received notification that the Home Office of the British and Foreign Bible Society had given authority for increase of my salary. Good news to me, coming unexpectedly as it did, but I only thought of it as beginning with that month. However, when the extra amount was given it included the increase from the month of March onward—again the very month I had kept my word to the Lord concerning this matter. Again I was impressed.

"The third year there was some delay, because of a mis-understanding on the part of the others about passing the money on, and a month or two passed before the money reached its destination. About the very day it was started on its way, a dear one in California sent me a special personal gift of money which came at a most opportune time.

"To be sure, one does not follow methods simply for the blessing they bring, but, knowing in such ways as these how God regards our gifts (so much so that He loves to bless in return), how good it is to have intimation of something which specially pleases Him!

"The friend who had opened my eyes to this matter had puzzled, because of this extreme in exchange—which came about the time I returned to China—about using so much Shanghai money to exchange for so few gold dollars to send to Jewish work, and, in this perplexity of mind, with the feeling it would be wrong to waste the Lord's money, had, with the other workers of her mission, hesitated and delayed for some time about the Jewish offerings, hoping for a more favorable exchange condition. In the meantime, the financial wheels had been dragging heavily. Money difficulties had come. While wondering if the Lord was satisfied with this delay, they heard my story, and the Lord arrested them. They saw that He was calling them definitely to return to their former practice in spite of conditions, for the silver and the gold were His. Immediately the Lord began to work; money came in: blessing was felt; and at the end of the year, in every branch of the accounts, there was a favorable balance. The year ended triumphantly.

"A family of six in Shanghai has recently adopted system-atic giving for Jewish work. One of the number, being employed in a publishing house, after making her first special gift toward this purpose, was later called in by her employer and informed that her salary had been increased. It was a liberal increase; and in these times of depression she could hardly fail to recognize God's blessing and connected it with her decision on this point. Other members of the family have also experienced special financial blessing.

"Need such instances be multiplied? It is certain that 'He who keepeth Israel shall neither slumber nor sleep,' and His heart is set upon the fulfillment of all His great promises to the Chosen People. He who overrules disasters and used the World War to accomplish His first great step toward their restoration, is watchful of each of our small contributions (whether by prayer or by gift) toward that great purpose established in the Heavens.

"For months the Spirit of the Lord has urged me to write about this matter. So I am passing it on for the consideration of others. Perhaps we have unconsciously reversed the Scriptures, making them read 'To the Greek first and also to the Jew.' Perhaps much may hinge upon our timely response to that which may be one of His last pressing thoughts in connection with the spread of the Gospel among the Jews, who are later to be the great evangelizers of the world."

And now, beloved friends, do not for a moment imagine that we are trying to offer you a short road to wealth! The fact that the Lord dealt in such remarkable ways with this missionary in Shanghai does not necessarily mean that He must deal in the same way with you or with me. It is not always money or material wealth that is a blessing; on the contrary, these things often are a curse. If He, in His inscrutable wisdom, sees fit to bring to any of His children material want and physical suffering, these may be the very things that He wants to use as a means of grace and blessing. The Israelites in the wilderness murmured, and clamored for meat. They thought that to fill their stomachs was of itself a blessing. But read the final verdict in Psa. 106:15, "He gave them their request; but sent leanness into their soul." Who of us would be willing to exchange fatness of soul for fatness of belly? You see, what really matters is that we as His children shall learn to do His will, and that fact of itself is a blessing.

With this we close. The past year has been a wonderful year of service for us in our Lord's world fields. Large undertakings lie before us for the months ahead. Your gifts, always so generously poured out to us in January, the first month of the year, are not only welcome and will be used for an aggressive pushing forward of the Gospel testimony; but, dear, dear, friends, the gifts are powerless, lifeless, unless they be energized by your earnest, believing, and beseeching prayers before the Throne of Grace. "They first gave their own selves to the Lord" is just as necessary today in Jewish missions, as it was nineteen hundred years ago when those poverty-stricken Macedonians gave their money to Paul. From the letters of our precious friends, we know this is true of our blessed Chosen People family. May it always be so.

"SALVATION IS OF THE JEWS"
January, 1938

The Preacher was wrong when he wrote in Ecclesiastes 1:10, "Is there anything whereof it may be said, See, this is new? it hath been already of old time, which was before us." In the previous verse the same poor Preacher, groping in his despair, and in the vain speculation of rational philosophy, makes another false statement, for he says, "The thing that hath been is that which shall be; and that which is done is that which shall be done and there is no new thing under the sun."

Dear friends, a new year is now with us; for the blind, heedless, lost world the new year is really not new; it is a going over of all that has been before, a continual mad merry-go-round. But to us into whose hearts God hath shined, to give the light of the knowledge of the glory of God in the face of Jesus Christ (II Cor. 4:6) there is truly something "new under the sun." We can prove to our fullest satisfaction that the Preacher was wrong; for we know experimentally the blessed truth of II Cor. 5:17 "Therefore if any man be in Christ, he is a new creature; old things are passed away; behold, all things are become new."

A New Thing In The Earth

It was God Himself, in collaboration with His only begotten Son, the Lord Jesus Christ, Who startled the world when He announced through the prophet Jeremiah, "The Lord hath created a new thing in the earth, A woman shall compass a man." And so that New Thing came to this earth, born of a virgin, thus truly the seed of woman as promised in Genesis, and through that New Thing, we now behold another new thing, that we have been born again and are become new creatures in Him. And so to us all things are become new, and His blessings and mercies to us are new and fresh every day.

Then He has also promised another new thing under the sun. This new thing we have not yet seen fulfilled as we have seen the other things fulfilled, in the coming of the Seed, and then in our own regeneration. But this new thing is still in the future, and it forms the very backbone of our holy faith. It is none other than the sure promise, "I will come again, and receive you unto myself; that where I am, there ye may be also." John 14:3. It is this coming again which is the blessed hope of every child of God, and which is the only answer to a world now in the agonizing throes of collapse. And when that new thing comes, what joy it will bring to the child of God who has patiently labored for his Lord down here, waiting so eagerly for that hallelujah shout, which will summon us to His presence where we shall be released from all care and sorrow and heartache and anxiety, and shall reign with Him for ever and ever.

Our Only Hope

This is the hope to which we who are united in the fellowship of His yearning over Israel, confidently look. And because of this hope and prize that is set before us, we labor on, seeking to win the lost sheep of the House of Israel back to the good Shepherd of the flock; one by one we seek them, even as the Shepherd seeks, and has always sought. And one by one He gathers them in, and they become new creatures, members of His blessed Body, also awaiting that glad shout. We fully realize that our great longing for that wonderful day will be the more quickly realized when the last one of that mysterious remnant of the House of Israel spoken of in

Romans 11:5, shall be brought into His church, and that church shall be complete.

And because this is the month of January we find ourselves almost under necessity to fall back on the usual custom of these many years, and give to our friends just a few repeated words of encouragement by way of re-affirmation and re-confirmation of the truth for which this Mission has stood for nearly fifty years, that the Gospel must be presented by the Church to the world, in only one order that the Scriptures recognize, to the Jew first. This is the bedrock doctrinal position we took nearly fifty years ago; we were at first ridiculed, sneered at, bullied; but the years have proven that the Word of God abideth forever and that he that doeth the will of God abideth forever. Our pioneer doctrinal foundation has stood the test of time, and now a host innumerable is praising the Lord with us for this revelation of truth that we have stood for persistently and sometimes obstinately, through the years of opposition and persecution. In other words, God has kept His word with us and He has vindicated our trust in Him and in His promise. When we took this position we determined that we would as it were nail our flag to the masthead, and we would never strike the colors, but we would stay with the ship whether it floats or sinks. And, lo and behold, now not only are there many, many friends praising the Lord with us, but there have also arisen many other efforts to evangelize the Jews, and these have taken hold of our pioneer watchword, so that we hear on all sides the shouts of these new comers, "To the Jew first! To the Jew first." For this of course we also give praise to the Lord Jesus Christ, for certainly the Church is in desperate need of an awakening to this important truth as to God's purposes in the present age for missionary undertakings.

"Let The Redeemed Say So"

We have thought that for a change our readers would enjoy the testimonies of other Christian leaders with regard to this precious Scripture truth. It is all very well for us to keep repeating these things to our readers, and we have been humbled to realize how graciously and trustfully our friends have rejoiced to see these things eye to eye with us. And we have felt that it is necessary that these truths be repeated over and over again: you remember how the writer in the Epistle to the Hebrews, speaking of the wonders and glories of the Person of the Lord Jesus Christ, reminds us, "Therefore we ought to give the more earnest heed to the things which we have heard, lest at any time we should let them slip." (Hebrews 2:1). But, it also helps much when we bring the force of outside testimony into the picture, for in this way there are others who reinforce and confirm the things we have been trying to say to you. So let us give you just a handful of some of the mature and sober judgments of men of God, men who have justly earned the respect and confidence of all of us who name His name. We start with that pioneer soul of Great Britain, Rev. John Wilkinson, of sacred memory, who spent a lifetime in going up and down the British Isles preaching practically all the time from the one text, "To the Jew first." Hear him as he says in the special quotation in "Trusting and Toiling" entitled, "The Divine Plan":

"God says 'First to the Jew,' and He will never alter it. And if we wish to have His blessing we must have it in obedience to Him, and we must alter our ways to His ways, and we must not wish Him to alter His ways to ours. The world will never be evangelized without the Jew. You may have your missionary conferences and your missionary meet-

ings all over the world, but if the Bible be the Word of God
you will never get the world evangelized without the Jew.
In the interest of the Gentile world then, go first to the Jew.
Put him in a prominent place in your prayers, and in your
efforts and in your practical sympathies, and you will get
blessing, for you will be on the lines of the Divine Plan."

We next take an excerpt from a present day warrior who
has been untiring and self-sacrificing in his courageous battle
against anti-Semitism in America. We refer to our beloved
brother, Rev. Keith L. Brooks, editor of Prophecy Magazine,
of Los Angeles. In a recent article in this magazine under
the heading of, "Christ's Most Unpopular Statement," Mr.
Brooks writes:

" 'Salvation is of the Jews.' (Jn. 4:22). These are the
words of Jesus Christ; words pregnant with meaning for
these days, but lightly waved aside by many. Dr. Walter M.
Wilson in a recent article in *Advent Witness,* comments:
'Salvation is always through two Jews; the one who wrote
the story in the Scriptures, and the One to whom the story
directs the seeker. Paul the Jew points the seeking soul to
Jesus the Jew. Peter the Jew directs the hearts of his hearers
to Christ the Jew. Salvation comes through hearing what one
Jew in the Bible says about the other Jew on the Cross and
on the Throne. There may be religions without the Jews, but
there cannot be salvation; there may be great church edifices
and a multitude of ardent worshippers without the Jews, but
these will have no salvation and never will join the blood-
washed throng in Glory. There may be beautiful thoughts,
kind acts and deeds, much of beneficence and bounty without
the Jews, but there can be no redemption, no forgiveness,
and no salvation apart from Israel; for salvation is of the
Jews. Those who reject the Jews, hate them, despise them,

and persecute them, shut the door of salvation for themselves and seal their own doom. This poor, sinsick, suffering, sorrowing earth will have no salvation in a national way until the Jews come into their own. When the Jews have their land again, and that greatest of all, *the peerless Jew,* the Lord Jesus Christ, is upon His throne in Jerusalem, then the earth will be saved from its throes and its woes; sighing will cease, and songs of praise will surge through the soul. Tears will be wiped away, and trials and troubles will be no more. This salvation is "of the Jews." In view of these facts we should certainly show our gratitude by doing something toward winning the Jew to Christ.' "

Let us turn to another saint who has long since departed and is now in the presence of his Lord, that late giant in the Scriptures, a missionary hero of Africa, Andrew Murray. Let us listen while he speaks to us out of the past:

"Pray for the Jews. Their return to the God of their fathers stands connected, in a way we cannot tell, with wonderful blessing to the Church, and with the coming of the Lord Jesus. Let us not think that God has foreordained all this, and that we cannot hasten it. In a divine and mysterious way God has connected His fulfillment of His promise with our prayer. His Spirit's intercession in us is God's forerunner of blessing. Pray for Israel and the work done among them, and pray too, 'Amen. Even so, come, Lord Jesus!' Isn't it marvelous that God condescends to hear and answer prayer? 'To you therefore, who believe, is the preciousness.' "

Now just a few words of poetry written by a devoted sister in the Lord, Mrs. H. S. Lehman, to whom God gave a talent for writing hymns, and the music likewise. One afternoon she had become greatly burdened over the sad condition of Israel, and she asked the Lord to give her some definite message that would stir the Church to prayer and labor in Israel's behalf. The result was a beautiful hymn entitled, "What Are You Doing For Them?" We give you below one verse and with it the chorus:

"First to the Jew" was the order He gave:
First to the Jew came Jesus to save;
First to the Jew when sins He forgave:
What are you doing for them?

How Jesus loved them! but we have despised,
Forgotten, neglected, in scorn undisguised.
Think you to face Him and hear His "Well done!"
With Israel, His chosen, left dying alone?

Once more we turn to a saint who has gone on to Glory, the late Dr. Jonathan Goforth. We quote from an article which appeared in "The Jewish Era" last year under the heading, "To the Jew First":

"Our beloved Dr. Goforth has left behind him, to inspire and bless the Church of our Lord Jesus Christ, a countless wealth of precious memory in his incomparable messages. None is more priceless to the writer than the one quoted here: 'It MUST be to the Jew FIRST; that is God's order.' The occasion was the last time we saw him—when he was speaking one afternoon last year on things pertaining to the deeper spiritual life and testimony, in the Church of St. Andrew and St. Paul in Montreal. In a brief personal conversation we were privileged to have with him following the service, we asked if he shared our conviction that the Gospel should be given to the Jew first. Turning the dear sightless eyes heavenward—his characteristic attitude—his face was illuminated with that spiritual light by which one *sees* the face of Jesus Christ; and the great missionary to

China gave answer in these never-to-be-forgotten words:
'It *must* be to the Jew *first;* that is God's order.' Recalling
the incident to Mrs. Goforth since her husband's homegoing,
she said: 'Ah yes, he always had a great love for the Jews!' "

There are many more quotations that we have been
gathering together, but now the space limit is becoming exhausted and so we will stop with just one final quotation. This
time it will be from one who was among the truest and most
loving friends that the Jews of America ever had. We refer
to that man of God, mighty in the Scriptures, self-effacing
and humble, the late Dr. James M. Gray, who for over
thirty years shaped the destinies of that stronghold of the
Christian faith, the Moody Bible Institute of Chicago. It was
in the midst of a frenzied and blatant campaign of hate
against the Jews that began in this country only four or five
years ago, that Dr. Gray, shocked and grieved that such
things could happen in a land at least nominally Christian,
wrote the following words:

"I would tremble to be guilty of fomenting an uprising
against the Jews; not merely because I fear the law of the
land, but because I fear God. The Jews are His chosen
people. If the Bible be true, then the redemption of the human
race on this earth, through the atoning merits of Jesus Christ,
is ultimately to be brought about, not by the Church, as
the body of Christ, which has a different mission, but by the
nation of Israel. Let us do all we can by testimony and
prayer to preach the Gospel 'to the Jew First,' as we are
commanded to do, that we may by all means save some."

Beloved friends, need we say more? The old Mosaic law
as to testimony was "at the mouth of two witnesses, or at
the mouth of three witnesses, shall the matter be established."
(Deuteronomy 19:15). But we have marshalled before you

many witnesses, not only two, and not only three, but many. It is as though we presented, in the words of Hebrews 12, "a cloud of witnesses." The child of God will need no further urging, or proof, or instruction. Here it is, so clear that a ten year old child can grasp it. All we wish to do in closing is to say as we have been saying each January for a good many years past, "The Lord's treasury is open for His faithful followers to make their gifts in this beginning month of a new year, literally to the Jew first." This invitation has always been sufficient to fill our treasury in the very first month of the year and thus to give us momentum for the carrying on of the work throughout the entire year; it is the old proverb of getting off to a good start. Our policy has been always from the beginning never to go into debt. We spend the money for the carrying on of the work only as God sends it on to us. Sometimes our faith has not been large enough, and the Lord has rebuked us by sending us more, sometimes much more, than we had planned for. But when this has happened, we simply broadened our base and lengthened our lines for the year following, and we used the balance for a rapid expansion of the work, because we saw evidences that God wanted us to go forward much faster than our poor slow minds could comprehend. This is the only explanation for the way in which God is blessing this Mission, and sending friends to our help—He wants the Gospel to be promulgated speedily and in a world-wide reach to the Jews. It is more true today than it was yesterday, that the time is short, and what we do must be done with haste. It is the teaching and urgency of I Samuel 21:8, "the King's business required haste." We little dream how imperative this haste must be in God's eyes in these days. The tidal waves of world calamity and destruction are moving upon us with startling swiftness, and we think of those soul-gripping words of "The Battle Hymn of the Republic,"

> He has sounded forth a trumpet that shall never call
> "retreat,"
> He is searching out the hearts of men before His
> judgment seat,
> Be swift my soul, to answer Him; be jubilant my feet;
> Our God is marching on!

And now, beloved friends, may the new year bring something truly new to each one of us; to those who sit in the shadow of a great sorrow may there come comfort from above; to those upon beds of pain and sickness, may there come mighty deliverance and happy release; to men and women whose shoulders are stooped under the burden and heat of the day, driven with the anxieties of the struggle for life itself, may there come a blessed assurance that He is walking by our side, carrying the load with us, bearing the anxiety with us, enduring the heat of the day with us. And again, we must remember that we are just one year nearer the day when He shall come in clouds of glory and we shall be transported into the eternal haven, that harbor of peace and quiet, where the storm-tossed waves can never enter, and where we shall join with the celestial hosts in singing those blessed words of praise that shall never tire our lips nor weary our minds, "Unto Him that loved us, and washed us from our sins in His own blood, and hath made us kings and priests unto God and His Father; to Him be glory and dominion for ever and ever. Amen." This is the only hope worth our while for this year. May it truly be a lively hope within each one of us, a hope that shall keep us steadfast through every day of the year, so that we shall be living examples of the truth that we are indeed new creatures in Christ Jesus our Lord. Old things have passed away, all things are become new.

RE-AFFIRMING GOD'S METHOD
January, 1939

The Holy Spirit tells us in I Cor. 12:12, 13, "For as the body is one, and hath many members, and all the members of that one body, being many, are one body: so also is Christ. For by one Spirit are we all baptized into one body, whether we be Jews or Gentiles, whether we be bond or free; and have been all made to drink into one Spirit."

And in the 26th verse we are reminded, "And whether one member suffer, all the members suffer with it; or one member be honored, all the members rejoice with it."

We are impressed anew with these simple yet profound truths as we read the hundreds of letters that you have been rushing to us in this dark hour of Israel's world agony. "My heart bleeds as I read of what the Jews are going through." "I must lay my paper down, for the tears keep pouring out of my eyes, and can't stop." "We can only cry out, How long, oh Lord, how long?" These are samples of what the Lord's people are writing us these days, and they show how tender is the heart, and how responsive the conscience, of the one who has been truly baptized into the one Body, the Church of the Lord Jesus Christ. If only the Confessional churches of Germany had realized these verities five years ago, and defied Hitler when he ordered them to drive out their Jewish Christian members! If only they had told Hitler, "No! If one member suffer, all the members suffer with it!" Perhaps Martin Niemoller would not now be languishing his life away in a Nazi concentration camp. Who knows, but that such a bold defiance of Satan's cohorts might have resulted in a new welter of martyrs' blood. And the blood of the martyrs has ever been the seed of the Church. So what a revival might have come if only those churchmen had been faithful! It was a Scottish martyr who exclaimed, when led to the lighted fagots for his horrible death by burning, "Aye, and we shall light a fire tonight that shall kindle all Scotland!" And it did!

Your gifts have been generously poured out in this hour of need. And we thank God a thousand times that He has given us so loving a host of friends, who weep when we weep, and rejoice when we rejoice. Such a fellowship is from above—there is no other explanation.

We cabled immediate relief funds to Palestine, to Austria, and to Paris, France. Out of Germany we are now shut completely, our agents there either having been arrested, or having escaped to other lands. In Austria we can still function because our connections there are through Aryan affiliates.

In Paris is now to be found the vortex of the German Jewish suffering, so far as we are affected. The city swarms with new refugees that some way have smuggled their way across the frontiers. Our Mission is now well known there, and our workers write us heartrending reports of tragedy upon tragedy. In this issue, we print some of these reports, so you may see the picture for yourself. More money we will keep sending, but always trying to use the best judgment God gives us. Most of these funds are given to Christian Jews, for they have first claim upon us—we are members of one body. But a good number of our contributors seem to have been led to state in their letters quite explicitly, "You must not restrict my gift to believing Jews only—give to all who come to you for help." So we do that too.

We are holding substantial sums of money on hand, so as to make possible a more even distribution month by month; and we also must have funds available if and when any workable plan of colonization is developed. So far, we cannot report more than that the whole subject is still under study and advisement. This is a case where we must make haste slowly. But be assured that your funds are being given the most careful and far-sighted administration.

As I write these lines a letter has come from our brother, Dr. Frank, with whom we have been carrying on negotiations concerning the Ecuador project. We will quote from his letter because we want you to get a look behind the scenes and understand better how intricate are the problems that must be solved even in what appears a simple matter of rooting up a few Jewish families and transplanting them:

"It is very sad and painful to read the numerous letters I get daily from suffering brethren in Germany. In many cases the Government has taken house and home, and their only hope is that we may be able to prepare their way into a foreign country. This, alas, is a very slow and difficult work; even though we have the land promised to us in Ecuador, it takes a great deal of time not only to select the people but to make the necessary arrangement for them prior to their immigration. Weeks pass too quickly; in the meantime the hope of those who are waiting is sinking; and yet one cannot send out a batch without sufficient preparation. An experienced Jewish Christian inspector of farms, and a medical man who knows Spanish fluently, are to go first, and after examining the place are to let us know how many families to send. But these two men, who are to do the pioneer work, are just now in the concentration camps, and although they have the permit they have not been released yet."

And so, dear friends, we need to be patient, and at the same time diligent. Just as fast as we can push any scheme for re-settlement, we will be in the front line, the Lord helping us.

Re-Affirming God's Method

And now a few words in season: It is once more the first month of a new year, and once more we follow the tradition and custom that has grown up with us these many years, of calling the attention of our family of readers to God's method in world-wide missions. How many mistakes, and how many tragedies have come into the world only because of original failure to put first things first. From the very foundation of this work, forty-four years ago, we felt led to establish it upon the one rock, as revealed in the Scriptures, "To the Jew first." And in those beginning days, what prejudice and opposition and even hatred, we had to face! But on we kept, knowing of a surety in our own souls, that we were doing God's work in God's way, "To the Jew first," and that God was bound, for His own honor's sake, to vindicate such a work and such a program.

The Lord Himself told us, "Salvation is of the Jews." John 4:22. It is true of course also, as Jonah found out in his leisure moments in the belly of the fish, that "Salvation is of the Lord." Jonah 2:9. It is pertinent to notice that Jonah was pretty well down in the mouth, and that only when he realized that salvation is of the Lord, did he come up smiling; for "the Lord spake unto the fish, and it vomited out Jonah upon the dry land." And then it was the same Jonah, a Jew, or to be more correct, a Hebrew, who went out to that great Gentile city of Nineveh, and preached the Gospel, and lo and behold, Nineveh repented and was saved! And so, salvation came from the Lord and salvation also came from the Jew, Jonah. All of which means, what if God has declared that only through a redeemed Israel shall come salvation to the world? Dare any human being join issue with God, or question His wisdom or His purpose? Is it not the question of Paul in Romans 9:20, "Who art thou that repliest against

God? Shall the thing formed say to him that formed it, Why hast thou made me thus?" If God has once and for all declared that only as Israel is blessed, so can the rest of the world be blessed, why quarrel with God? Why not rather co-work with Him? The whole program is reduced to the one contingency, that the sooner the Jew is brought to Christ, the sooner a whole world will be converted, for that Jew, reborn, will be as Paul tells us in Romans 11, "Life from the dead."

The Privilege Imperative

"To the Jew first." Was there ever a time in the world's history when this precious privilege was more imperative than in this present hour? With Israel in the cauldron of demon hate, with the world being driven by Satan himself, to exterminate, if that were possible, the people whom God has called His very own, can any true child of God evade the implications and the necessities of a ministry in such an hour as this, "To the Jew first"? Ought we not, while He still tarries, reach out in a labor of love to this sorely harassed and distressed people, who know not which way to turn? "To the Jew first" indeed has a potent meaning on this Saturday night of world history.

"To the Jew first." What agony of soul and body might have been averted in Germany, for instance, if the Church of Christ had faithfully preached and practiced this doctrine for the last two hundred or three hundred years! It is only as the child of God is properly steeped in Bible knowledge concerning the Jew, that he learns to know how dear to the heart of God is the seed of Abraham. And once a child of God understands this, and retains also the fear of God in his heart, he cannot dare bring himself to raise a finger or to wag a tongue against Israel, "beloved for the fathers' sakes."

But here is the tragedy, that Jew-hate invariably links itself up, or terminates with, hatred for God and hatred for God's Word. This is exactly what we have witnessed across the water in these last few years. The first step of Satan was to build up an anti-Semitic party in Germany; the next step was to develop throughout Germany the demon hate for the Jew; and now finally the serpent has revealed his fangs; for the true objective of Satan is not so much to destroy the Jew, as it is to destroy God's Word. He finds the Jew an obstacle in his plan, and so the first thing to do is to get the Jew out of the way. Then comes the real blow and that is directed at the Word itself. For see what has been the latest happening in Germany: Under the new laws, promulgated only two or three weeks ago, the word Jehovah must be stricken out of all Bibles, the name of every Hebrew prophet must be eliminated, and if any pastor disobeys these orders, and dares to mention the name of Jehovah in the church, or the name of a Hebrew prophet, the church will be burned as were the synagogues during those days of nightmare early in November, when Germany became almost a shambles for Jewish blood and Jew hate. So, dear reader, if you treasure for yourself the Word of God, and if it has any precious value to your soul, then by all means remember to put the Jew in your missionary perspective exactly where God has put him, "first."

Fatalism Is Fatal

"To the Jew first." The sure word of Prophecy tells us that in spite of all that we will be able to do in our effort to stem the tide of Jew hate, the devil will succeed just the same, but only to the extent of a stirring of Jew hate to the point of bringing on the time of Jacob's trouble, such a time of torture and agony as Israel has never known before. But it will not do for us to hide behind such an alibi by say-

ing, "Well it has been so prophesied, and the Jew is getting what is coming to him." The rather arresting truth must be brought home to every child of God who in such an hour as this blunders his way into this sort of philosophy, that God will never hold guiltless one human being who will dare to raise a hand of affliction or persecution against the Jew. There is coming a day of reckoning, a time of accounting, a time when God's fury shall come into His face, and He will avenge the wrongs done toward His own covenant people. That is why we shudder when we think of what men like Hitler will have to face in the day of judgment. The prophecy contained in Matthew 25:31-46 is of special application now. It will be to men like Hitler that the Lord will soon say, "I was a stranger, and you took me not in, naked and ye clothed me not, sick and in prison, and ye visited me not. . . . Verily I say unto you, inasmuch as ye did it not to one of the least of these (my brethren) ye did it not to me. And these shall go away into everlasting punishment." If we are in the early rumblings of the swiftly onrushing hour of Jacob's trouble, and if the time is close at hand when God will judge the nations for their treatment of the Jews, then again by all things that are sacred and precious and life-giving, we owe it to God and to ourselves, and to our future welfare, to go with the Gospel "To the Jew first."

"To the Jew first." What blessed memories stir the hearts of all of us as we think back and remember that to Israel "pertaineth the adoption, and the glory, and the covenants, and the giving of the law, and the service of God, and the promises . . . and of whom as concerning the flesh Christ came, who is over all, God blessed for ever." Romans 9:4, 5. If ever you and I get to heaven and sing the glory song of the redeemed in that celestial chorus that shall continue its arias into an endless eternity, it will be because a Holy

God took upon and in Himself the body and the flesh and the blood of a Jew, and tabernacled with us here on this earth, and then went to Calvary and there poured out with measureless abandon, the most precious blood that ever coursed through the veins of a human body. If ever we understand the consoling doctrines, profounder than all the brains of the world's philosophers put together, of the vicarious atonement, the just for the unjust, of sins forgiven, of eternal peace made with God, of daily protection and guidance by the Holy Spirit, of the sureness of our Lord's coming to take us up to be with Him in the air, if ever we grasp the fullest meanings of these divine realities, it will be because a Jew, Saul by name, one day met his Lord face to face, and heard the heartbreaking accusation, "Saul, Saul, why persecutest thou me?" Having heard that, that Jew became Paul, the greatest missionary the world ever saw; and that Paul gloried in the fact that he had been called out to give the Gospel to the Gentiles. Let us remember that it was this Paul who sewed tents that he might make his living so that he could preach the Gospel to the Gentiles without charge to them. In short, ordinary gratitude dictates now in the hour of Israel's agony, that the child of God shall go with a Gospel ministry of love and sympathy, "To the Jew first." It will not do to hide behind the shameful propaganda of the present hour which tries to tell us that Judaism is synonymous with Communism. This is about as Satanic a falsehood as ever came from human lips. Certainly there are Jews who are Communists; and there are Jews who are Republicans, and Jews who are Democrats, and Jews who are believers in the Lord Jesus Christ. Paul parries this question when he puts forth the challenge in reply to the accusation that all the Jews did not accept the Lord Jesus Christ. "What if some did not believe? Shall their unbelief make the faith of

God without effect? God forbid." Romans 3:3. The present day propaganda that Judaism is Communism, is one of those last desperate thrusts of the devil to turn away the mind and eyes of the child of God from the one commission and privilege that has been given to the Church in these days, to maintain a ministry of the Gospel, "To the Jew first."

Before The Ship Sinks

"To the Jew first." Brethren, we are in the last days. From uncounted millions of weary hearts throughout this world there goes up the daily cry, "Even so, come Lord Jesus!" And suppose He should come before you finish reading these very lines, do you know anything that would please Him more than for you to be able to say to Him, "I have loved thy people, I have yearned for them as thou didst yearn over them when thou wast here upon the earth. I have prayed for them, I have given of my substance that they might know about salvation through Thy precious blood." In other words, if there is in your heart a genuine love for the Lord Jesus Christ, your Saviour, then it follows as surely as night follows day, that there must also be a love for those whom He called "My brethren"; and such a love makes itself manifest by a strict adherence to the command that He gave, "To the Jew first."

Behold, I Stand And Knock

And so once more, as we have done for many years past in the month of January, we say to our beloved friends, the treasury of the Lord is now open to receive in this, the first month of a new year, the earnest of your determination to carry on God's work in God's way, "To the Jew first." It has come to be an ingrown custom with our precious Chosen People family, to set aside faithfully, conscientiously and literally, the first offerings of the New Year, to be used for the Lord's Gospel, "To the Jew first." Certainly this year presents the need and the opportunity in a way that transcends in importance any year since the Lord put us on this field forty-four years ago. What is in store for us, no man living dare foretell, or can foresee. An array of symptoms the world over, if set down on these pages now, line by line, would make us all feel rather weird and eerie; for such a procession of fact after fact would form a cavalcade of such heart shaking proportions that we would understand with a clearer comprehension the meaning of the solemn words of our Lord, "It is near, even at the doors."

We are closing December as the largest December in our history, financially, and we give God thanks, and take courage. Shall we have the month of January just a bit better than December, so that we shall allocate our funds and then undertake a program, across the water, of genuine and far reaching relief to those who sit in the shadows of great sorrow and grief? All of this, in addition to carrying on the regular Gospel programs of our stations both here in the homeland and in our foreign centers.

We cannot close without expressing the earnest wish and prayer for each of our friends for the Lord's grace to be made manifest to you during this new year. It is a year that holds many possibilities. May we be found faithful, and may we be filled with the sense of His own presence, being always conscious, even though our souls be tried as it were by fire, that the eternal God is our refuge and that underneath us and around us are the Everlasting Arms. It was Moses the man of God who blessed Benjamin in Deut. 33:12, with these gracious words:

The beloved of Jehovah shall dwell in safety by Him;
He covereth him all the day long,
And he dwelleth between His shoulders.

Yea, He loveth the people;
All His saints are in Thy hand:
And they sat down at Thy feet;
Every one shall receive of Thy words.

May this be your experience in the midst of a world filled with confusion and fear, and revolution against God.

A BASIC DOCTRINE

January, 1940

The secret of successful pedagogy lies in constant repetition. The reason why the rising generation is so superficial is because there was absent in its younger days those hours of drudgery which our grandfathers knew—hours of repetition, repetition, and repetition. Catechism, Bible, Psalter, these were the essentials of the days of our grandfathers; and what sturdy characters were produced! And that is why the Psalmist so beautifully says of the good man, "In His law doth he meditate day and night." That is why God told Israel, "Thou shalt teach them (the commandments) diligently unto thy children." Deut. 6:7.

And that is why we come to you again with the reminder which we have so often brought to you in former issues, that the Gospel order is still "to the Jew first." This doctrine has been the foundation upon which this Mission has predicated its existence from the day of its inception. This work was begun because of an earnest and unshakable conviction that the Bible doctrine of "to the Jew first" is just as imperative today as it was on the day it was first uttered; that this doctrine is as basic in its application to the missionary program of the Church, as faith in Christ is basic in the program of salvation. Upon this conviction this work stands or falls. There have been no sentimental appeals in connection with this Mission, no artificial means used for securing funds, no questionable methods employed, no paid staff of campaign managers. Our sole reliance has been upon the belief that the Word of God cannot return unto Him void; that there must be in this country a sufficient number of the Lord's people to whom a "thus saith the Lord" means implicit obedience. To such a constituency we have resolutely and persistently addressed ourselves through all these years, having felt that if once such Christians were convinced that the Word of God says, "to the Jew first," then of course it must be so, and there can be no further question about it.

This Is a Scripture-Obeying Enterprise

The results, as now apparent after many years of this sort of indoctrinating, have proven beyond a doubt that a scriptural appeal made to the heart and mind of a Scripture-loving child of God, will produce abundant support for a Scripture-obeying enterprise such as we always want the American Board of Missions to the Jews to be. The results have been that year after year the friends whom the Lord has given to us have continued faithful in their loyal and generous support of the work, not because of any persuasion, not because of any emotion, but because the Word of God has, by virtue of repetition and repetition and repetition, sunk deep into the hearts and has become a part of them so that they can no more help giving of their means "to the Jew first," than a bird can help flying. It is as a bubbling fountain of refreshing water; the quality of the water never changes because it is inherent at the source. So a Christian who has been truly steeped in the Word of God has become indeed a fountain of living water from which there flows continually refreshing streams to a dry and thirsty land.

In re-echoing to you this year this old but ever-important doctrine, we thought that you would be interested in reading a letter we wrote to a friend of the Mission some months ago; this friend took exception to our teaching in regard to the Gospel order of "to the Jew first" and we wrote her concerning these objections point by point. We were gratified later to hear from this friend that the letter was a great help to her and on that account we thought that perhaps there are many others of our readers who would be helped by such a letter; so we have condensed it somewhat and now quote from it as follows:

With reference to your question as to the doctrine of "to the Jew first";—If we are to accept the interpretation which you give, that in the epistles, "to the Jew first," no longer holds, then how are we to explain such a passage as Romans 1:16? Or Romans 2:9-10? This latter passage deals with future punishment and has yet to be fulfilled.

You quote Acts 13:46, "Lo, we turn to the Gentiles," but you apparently did not notice, in the chapter immediately following, Acts 14:1, that when they went into the next town, Iconium, they went again "to the Jew first." It is a matter of principle, for in Acts 13:46, Paul says, "it was *necessary* that the word should *first* have been spoken to you." This gives us a clear insight into God's divine order, that we owe the Gospel message "to the Jew first" regardless of whether he will hear or will not hear. I heard a good answer given by a banker to a Christian brother who resented the doctrine of "to the Jew first." This banker simply turned to him and asked, "In what age are we living now?" The other answered immediately, "In the church age, of course." The next question the banker asked was, "In what age did Paul write Romans 1:16?" The other answered, "In the church age." "Then there you have your answer," said the banker, "for God never changes His plans in any given dispensation; whatever was true in the days when Paul wrote the Epistle to the Romans, is just as true this very moment, for it is one and the same dispensation."

There Is No Difference

You quote Romans 10:12, "For there is no difference

between the Jew and the Greek: for the same Lord over all is rich unto all that call upon Him"; but are you not mis-applying Scripture? Paul is here speaking specifically con-cerning the method by which a person becomes a child of God in the present age of election; by that method, which is through individual faith in the Lord Jesus Christ, the same God is rich unto all that call upon Him; furthermore this same teaching is given later on in the epistle when it has to do with the Church; in the Church there is neither Jew nor Greek, we are all one in Christ. If you and I are members of the same Church body, we are both children of God and there is not the slightest preference to be given to me because I am a Jewish Christian; we are both one in Christ. But the Lord does make a very clear distinction as to the peoples outside of the Church, as you will notice in 1 Cor. 10:32, "Give none offence, neither to the Jews, nor to the Gentiles, nor to the Church of God." Here we have clearly stated that there are three classes of peoples in the world, Jews, Gentiles and Christians.

The Christian is given instructions by God how to bring the message of His salvation to the world. Just imagine that the Church stands by herself on the mountain top and sees below her the huge masses of peoples; the Church, counting herself out from the world, will see only two classes, Jews and Gentiles. Now the Lord's instruction to the Church is to evangelize the whole world, but she must do it by giving the Gospel "to the Jew first" and then to the Gentile. It does not mean that the Jew is better than the Gentile, nor that the Jew even has preference over the Gentile, it simply means that it is God's order. Perhaps I can illustrate it more clearly by referring to the making of a fire in the kitchen stove: We know that the proper *order* for making a fire is first to put in the grate some paper, and on top of the paper some light pieces of wood, then a little heavier wood, and then finally coal. This method will produce a fire. But supposing that one were to say, "I do not like this order, putting the paper in first. I think I will put the coal in first, and then the wood and then the paper." You can readily see that there would be no permanent fire built on that basis. At the same time nobody claims that the paper is better than the coal, it simply has to be put into the grate *first* and it has to serve its purpose first. The same truth applies to the question of "To the Jew first." There is a peculiar function which the Lord wants the Jew to perform and that is why He has given the command "To the Jew first." That the Church has refused to obey this command for these last two thousand years is a matter of serious loss to herself and of incalculable grief to our Lord Jesus Christ.

"I Say The Truth In Christ"

To Paul was revealed a glimpse of the importance of this doctrine; so important indeed did he realize it to be, that he was impelled to say in Romans 9:1, 3, "I say the truth in Christ, I lie not, my conscience also bearing me witness in the Holy Ghost ... I could wish that myself were accursed from Christ for my brethren." When Paul calls upon the things most sacred in life with which to enforce the teaching as to the importance of Jewish evangelization, it is surely sufficient reason for us in these days to follow his example, for as he himself says, this revelation was given to him by God Himself, and is not merely a matter of patriotism.

Finally, I have asked many objectors to this doctrine of "To the Jew first," among them ministers of wide knowledge, to show me a single passage in the Bible which definitely cancels the instruction that the Gospel should be given "to the Jew first." I have never found one person who gave me a satisfactory answer to this question. It surely is reasonable to expect that when God gives space in the Bible to such a positive phrase as "to the Jew first" He would give equal space to an equally positive cancelling; but all such contrary instruction is lacking, and in the face of this lack I am satisfied in my own mind, and there are thousands of earnest Christians who are likewise satisfied, that the divine method of missions is today as it was two thousand years ago, "to the Jew first." It will not do to argue that the Jews had the Gospel first, for that argument is specious; I can counter such argument by saying that the Gentiles also had the Gospel, therefore we ought not to go to the Gentiles either. The only logical and fair conclusion is that we owe the Gospel to the Jew first here in our generation; God will not excuse us from our obligation now in the present day and age simply because we point to an incident two thousand years ago when some Jews in some particular town through some particular apostle did have the Gospel "to the Jew first." That does not help to bring salvation to the Jew of today. The whole summing up of the matter is, simply, that in every generation the Church must give the Gospel to the whole world, but in that particular order "to the Jew first," and then to the Gentile; and then keep repeating this over and over again in each succeeding generation.

There Is An Awakening

Be it said, with profound thanksgiving, that year after year the Lord is permitting us to witness an increasing number of Christian people who are awaking to this long-forgotten teaching. Even as we go to press we are receiving scores of letters, all of them telling us in effect, "I am sending you my first offering of the New Year, because I want to give this contribution 'To the Jew first.'" Many tell of remarkable blessings received because of obedience to the Lord in this matter. One such letter has come even as we are writing this editorial, and because it is typical of others we quote a few lines from it:

"I told you a few weeks ago that I would 'try the Lord' by doubling my subscription to your Mission. I must tell you that I think the Lord has made good already. For I got a letter the other day inclosing a post office order for $15.00 —being money I earned by teaching a young lady shorthand twenty years ago, but which she never paid for, and I had charged it to profit and loss long ago. It was an out-lawed-three-times-over-account, and I have written a somewhat lengthy letter to my pastor relating fully the facts, and telling him that I cannot but regard it as a direct answer to my test of God for His blessing."—*T. I. D.*

Dear friend, will you not join such a company? Will you not put God to the test for this year?

THREE MUSTS OF SCRIPTURE

January, 1941

"Study to show thyself approved unto God." This was the injunction given by Paul to his young son in the ministry, Timothy. And Paul proceeded to tell him how he could show himself approved. It was that he should be, "a workman that needeth not to be ashamed, rightly dividing the word of truth." And so the emphasis is stressed to the child of God on knowing correctly how to divide God's revealed truth. We read, "The entrance of thy words giveth light; it giveth understanding to the simple." Psalm 119:130. And the word "simple" has the meaning of a willing heart, an open mind, an eager desire to know God's will. It is only to such that God will reveal Himself.

A Sound Principle Of Exegesis

As far back as 1889, in his classic volume, "Israel My Glory," the sainted John Wilkinson of London, enunciated a valid principle of exegesis which has stood the test of time through the years. It reads as follows:

"The principle adopted in quoting Scripture to prove anything, past or future, is simply to let the Word of God mean what He says; that is, *if the plain and obvious make good sense, seek no other sense.*"

And this brings us to our point. For a good many years we have tried as best the Lord has enabled us, to set forth the place that God has reserved for Israel, His peculiar treasure, in His missionary program—to the Jew first. Since January is the first month of the year, we have given special emphasis to this basic principle of world-wide missions, in this month. And God has honored our practice, because more and more do our friends keep writing us especially in January, how dearly has this precious doctrine become attached to their hearts.

And so it is time again to speak of these things. But it is not so easy, year after year, to give this subject a fresh approach. It is true that many would be glad to have us repeat some of the expositions set forth in years gone by, while a good many others, being among the more recent additions to our beloved family of readers, never have even read the previous exhortations along these lines. And so we are "in a strait betwixt the two." At any rate, we can start at the basic point that already has been suggested, that whenever the Word of God gives a statement which in its literal sense makes good sense, then by all means let us accept it.

The Three Musts

In the general Kingdom truth as revealed in the Scriptures, we find three MUSTS, or three categorical imperatives, as the philosophers would have it, things indispensable as prerequisites for membership in the Kingdom of God.

1—There is the initiatory must—"Ye must be born again!" This is the entrance door to the Kingdom, there is no other. God can have no dealings with a sinner on any basis of sonship or family relationship until this first MUST has been complied with. It is a mystery. It has puzzled the greatest minds of history, and it has baffled the most brilliant brains. It puzzled Nicodemus, that educated ruler among the Jews, to whom the Lord Jesus Christ revealed this mystic requirement. And the Lord told him, "The wind bloweth where it listeth, and thou hearest the sound thereof, but canst not tell whence it cometh, and whither it goeth; so is every one that is born of the Spirit." John 3:8.

2—The second MUST finds its elucidation in such a passage as Acts 13:46, "It was necessary (a MUST, imposed by the inherent nature of the missionary task) that the Word of God should first have been spoken to you (Jews)." Additional light is thrown on this second MUST by the words of the Lord Jesus Christ in Matt. 15:24, "I am not sent but unto the lost sheep of the house of Israel."

How Can One Love The Jews?

In Scripture, a mystery is something divulged to a child of God, but he must first be a child of God before there shall be revealed to him any of the mysteries of the Kingdom. To use a poor comparison but the best one we can think of at the moment, it is like one who becomes a member of a secret society; it is only after he has become a member that the secrets and mysteries of the society are made known to him. This, in the secular world; but think how much more wonderful it is that God makes known to us who have been born again into His family, the mysteries of the Kingdom. Psalm 25:14 tells us, "The secret of the Lord is with them that fear him." When God once came to visit Abraham, He debated whether He should reveal to Abraham the secret of His purpose to destroy Sodom and Gomorrah. Now Abraham is the only man in all history who is called the Friend of God. And here, we suppose, God hesitated for a few moments, and then remembering His affectionate friendship for Abraham, He asked Himself the question, "Shall I hide from Abraham that thing which I do?" And to us who are also friends of the Lord Jesus Christ, and brethren, and fellow heirs with Him, there are given these progressive revelations of Kingdom truth. And, strangely enough, it is only those who are the closest friends of God, to whom He speaks through the still voice of His Holy Spirit who are the ones who respond to that voice, and do His bidding, without quibble or murmur. We might as well say frankly that one of the hardest things for the average person to do, is to love the Jews. It takes a born-again child of God to do that, a regenerated soul who has learned in the new life of Christ, to love what once it hated, and to hate what once it loved. Our files are crowded with letters testifying as to how the writers used to hate the Jews, but that after conversion their hatred was turned into love, and then God revealed to them His secrets, His purpose for Israel, and after that such a soul has found delight in showing love to that people.

3—"And he must needs go through Samaria." John 4:4. And now comes the final MUST, which reveals in searchlight brilliancy, the paramount reason why there is a MUST as to giving the Gospel to the Jew first. You will see in a moment that God's horizon is as wide as the universe itself, and that there is no mere petty tribal prejudice which lies behind His instructions. Christ must needs go by way of Samaria. Why? Because there was a poor Gentile woman that would be meeting Him at Jacob's well, to whom He must needs impart forgiveness of sins. The Jews normally would have no dealings with the Samaritans, but here the Lord Jesus Christ gave the first gleam of revelation concerning His future purpose for Israel's task in the world. And so, He had that searching conversation with the poor woman at the well. And the streams of blessing which flowed out of that interview we suppose will never be measured this side of eternity.

But here we have the adumbration of God's ultimate destiny for the redeemed remnant out of Israel. The Lord went to Samaria, and then we read, "The woman then left her waterpot, and went her way into the city, and saith to the men, Come, see a man, which told me all things that ever I did: is not this the Christ?" John 4:28, 29. And still farther down in the record we read, "And many of the Samaritans of that city believed on him for the saying of the woman, which testified, He told me all that ever I did." John 4:39. And so this thing which the Lord Jesus Christ did individually is the foreshadowing of what the Jewish nation will do when they will proclaim the Gospel to a world Samaria. It is only as Israel shall be converted that the world can be converted. There can never be world blessing apart from Jewish blessing—one is contingent on the other, and flows out of it inherently.

"There Is A Remnant—"

And so, if God has declared to His church a MUST, and has revealed a mystery, that the Gospel shall be given to the Jew first, are you going to quarrel with God about that? The late sainted Dr. D. M. Stearns, who spent many years as a Bible teacher, and to whom was given the great privilege of stressing the necessity for the Church to give the Gospel to the Jew first, wrote once in one of his printed sermons a few comments on Romans 1:16, "to the Jew first." Here are some of them:

"Were Paul to return to the earth today he would find as great need most earnestly to address to the churches the words of our text, as he had to write them to the Church at Rome. That we may no longer be ignorant of this mystery, let us humbly and prayerfully consider these words.... 'Let us not forget that there is a gathering of Israel now with which we have something to do.' There is 'a remnant according to the election of grace,' to be gathered to the Lord Jesus in this present time to form the Jewish portion of the Bride of Christ, and this remnant is to be gathered by the preaching of the Gospel."

And was ever a time more opportune for a ministry of
the Gospel, "To the Jew first"? A people scattered and
peeled, driven like cattle over the fields of Europe, beaten,
robbed, despoiled of everything precious in life, what a cry
they present to us who profess the name of the Lord Jesus
Christ! Even a wounded dog causes us to hurry to his help;
here in New York there is a law that an automobile driver
who happens to run over a dog, must stop immediately and
take the animal to a hospital. But here we face a people
numbering over ten millions who are in the position of that
injured and bleeding animal. May it never be said of us
that we had more pity for an animal than for the shattered,
desolate, and broken millions of the children of Israel! Could
anyone, with any kind of a heart, deny these people in the
present world crisis a ministry of the Gospel, "To the Jew
first"!

A Remarkable Testimony

And then there is of course the other side, the fact that
God does reward those who obey His basic command in
world-wide missions. We have printed many times the
testimonies of some of the Lord's choicest saints, proving
that God did bless them when they began to obey Him as
to His divine program in Missions, "To the Jew first." There
has come to our desk, however, a remarkable account written
in "The Harvester" by a brother beloved in the Lord, Mr.
L. M. Anglin, the head of the Home of Onesiphorus. He
takes for his theme the subject, to the Jew first, and then he
tells a remarkable story of God's faithful dealings with him
as a result of his faithfulness to God concerning Israel. We
have room for only a few condensed paragraphs:

"In 1936, I was again reminded by the Spirit about our
obligation to the Jews in the way of giving of our means and

praying for them. I had always felt, since my call to China, that I owe my time, strength and prayers to China, and both myself and my wife have given all we have for China. I did not feel that I had anything more to give to others since I had given all to the Lord for the dear Chinese. At that time my wife was seriously ill and we had very little of this world's goods, not even enough for our own needs at such a time as this. But the necessity of giving something regularly to the Jews was so heavily laid on my heart, I went out into the woods north of us and there in a secluded place I went over the matter in my mind and settled once for all that I would give a contribution to the work among the Jews in January and June of each year.

"For two or three years my wife and I had been getting a personal donation from a church in America, and I promised the Lord that I would give this check for the work among the Jews twice each year. Many months this was about all my wife and I would ever get (we do not have a salary, but receive free-will offerings for our own personal use) but I promised God that I would give this entire amount no matter whether we were in need or whether the children in the Home had no food.

"Soon after I made my promise, our check from this church came and if ever we needed money for the Home and for ouselves, we needed it then; but I was faithful to God in keeping my promise and sent the check immediately to the American Board of Missions to the Jews for their work.

"After this the Lord began to work in our behalf. My wife underwent a serious operation and when the doctors had decided that another operation was necessary to save the situation, the Lord came forth in one night's time, between the time of the doctor's decision and the time set for the operation the next morning, and completely delivered her from the dangerous symptoms. At once she began to improve, and to the surprise of all, was able to leave the hospital in three weeks, and go home, where she improved steadily each day.

"For more than a year we had been trying to raise passage funds to come to America but it seemed to come in so slowly. But after my wife came out of the hospital the Lord worked miracles and within a short while sufficient funds came in to enable us to come to America. It seemed that every cloud rolled away and the dear Lord was just pouring out blessings on us."

Our Two-Fold Ministry

A testimony of this kind surely is evidence enough of God's blessings upon any one of His children who will love Israel as He has loved them. And for forty-five years He has put us here and kept us here, that we might carry out a two-fold ministry; first, to give the Gospel, as Peter did in the apostolic days, to the scattered sheep of Israel; and then secondly, and equally important, to testify to the Church of Christ concerning God's covenant people. And from the beginning we were led to take our stand squarely upon the doctrine, "To the Jew first." We were laughed at, we were ridiculed, we were even hated, but our faces were set as flint, and we would not be moved. If we were wrong, then all Jewish Missions were wrong, and no Jew had any claim to the Gospel. If on the other hand there was a place in the Church program for the Jew; then that place could only be in the Scriptural order, to the Jew first. Upon that platform we decided we would stand unmoved, and God has seen fit to bless that testimony, and every year He is giving us ever increasing evidences of His blessings on our efforts. And every January there is always a larger number of His choicest children who send their gifts literally in the first month of the new year, "To the Jew first." And this of course gives your Mission a boost with which to start the new year, and we know how to plan our budgets, and keep out of debt.

And so, beloved friends, may we now say that the treasury is open once more that you may cast in your gifts, "To the Jew first." You need no urging, for many times have our hearts been melted with your sacrificial generosity. All we need to say is, the doors are open.

For the new year, may we give to you the warmest greeting of our hearts; what the year holds in store, no human being knows. We do know that we are very near the brink of cataclysm, and for us that only makes brighter the hope of our redemption, and down in our hearts there echoes the plea of that sainted seer of Patmos, "Even so come Lord Jesus."

FOR JONATHAN'S SAKE

January, 1942

It is the last month of the year, as we write these lines for the January issue. We cannot enter now into retrospect of what the year has brought to us as your Jewish Mission, because we propose to do this in February when we recount all the ways in which our God has led us.

We project ourselves into the month of January, and we realize it is a new year and the first month of the new year. What it holds in store, He alone knows, He who "hath put the times and the seasons in His own power." Acts 1:7. From the burden of the letters which reach us day by day, we know only too well how the hearts of His most faithful ones are yearning with "groanings which cannot be uttered" for that long hoped-for day, when He shall descend from the clouds with that final shout that shall bring grateful release to millions of souls now in the agonies of such sorrows as the world has not known since the sun began to shine. It is of that which the Holy Spirit reminds us in Romans 8:22, as actually now occurring throughout the world,

"For we know that the whole creation groaneth and travaileth in pain together until now."

What a wonderfully blessed day that will be when the longings of a lifetime will suddenly come to their denouement, in that brilliant hour when He shall literally rend the skies and come to take us to be with Him in those heavenly mansions which even now He is preparing for our eternal abode! It is to that end that we, together with our many precious friends, have labored unitedly in His Vineyard these past twelve months; for to us has been given the revelation out of the Word of God itself, that there is no surer way to hasten that glad hour of world expectancy, than to devote our every energy to the evangelizing of His scattered but still beloved people Israel. The thorough impregnation of the Jewish nation with the seed of Gospel teaching, this is the final prelude to that event which will result in the fulfillment of Zech. 14:4, "And his feet shall stand in that day upon the Mount of Olives." Perhaps these very persecutions through which the Jews of the world are now passing, make the opportunity for the true child of God to evangelize as never before, and we may be nearer the fulfillment of Joel 2, than we think, when as the last shower of God's blessings upon Israel and as the last testimony to a world of unbelief, there shall come a Pentecostal revival upon Israel, and there will be fulfilled the stirring promise of Joel 2:28, "I will pour out my spirit upon all flesh; and your sons and your daughters shall prophesy, your old men shall dream dreams, your young men shall see visions."

On The Threshold

Certainly God is giving us here in our own Headquarters Building signs that such a Pentecostal blessing is in the making, for the refugee Jews come to us, tender hearted, broken in spirit, and eager to know what is the mind of the Lord, and in the spirit of Paul of old many are asking, "Lord what wilt thou have me to do?" Our blessed privilege it is to lead these wandering souls into the haven of rest, through the peace once for all made possible through our Lord Jesus Christ and His atoning work at Calvary.

Once More God's Order

But now it is January again, the first month of a new year, and for a good many years past we have never let

January slip by without saying something in these pages
about God's divinely ordained order in Missions, "To the
Jew first." It has become a sort of fixture with us, and the
people of our blessed family rather expect it. Not that they
have any doubt about it, for certainly the events of these last
few years have piled evidence upon evidence as to the
eternal truth of this foundation doctrine in Missions. But,
we all enjoy once in a while a fresh recital of the reasons
for the faith within us, and so many of our friends love to
dwell upon this precious revelation that God has given them,
through a faithful study of His Word, that the Gospel order,
"To the Jew first," is still in force and has never been cancelled by God. Those who obey this order find rich blessings,
and experience new depths of God's grace in their own lives,
and they never seem to feel more close to God, than when
they are engaged in meditation upon the Jewish question,
and in prayer to God, "that Israel might be saved." And such
a deep-rooted conviction, coming from God alone, is the only
explanation for the way in which God has blessed your
Mission and has crowned its every effort with so many
tokens of His pleasure.

For Jonathan's Sake

Our minds have been dwelling much lately as we have
been pondering this January message, on the beautiful story
contained in II Sam. 9. It is a bit difficult, of course, year
after year, to bring a message on a "To the Jew first" text,
and always to have the message fresh. Repetition in a case
of this sort cannot be avoided, and must be expected, and
allowed for. Repetition furthermore is a good thing, for all
didactic methods are based on this one fundamental pedagog-
ic principle: repeat, repeat, repeat. So our friends have been
very patient with us and long-suffering, and we have always

thanked God for that, for after all we are only human, and prone to all the shortcomings and weaknesses of the flesh.

But now to come to II Sam. 9, where we read that David enquired, "Is there yet any that is left of the house of Saul, that I may show him kindness for Jonathan's sake?"

And they found one called Mephibosheth, the son of Jonathan, the son of Saul, and the record goes on to say:

"David said unto him, Fear not: for I will surely shew thee kindness for Jonathan thy father's sake." II Sam. 9:7.

And later on we get in the closing verse of the chapter the final picture as the curtain drops.

"So Mephibosheth dwelt in Jerusalem; for he did eat continually at the king's table; and was lame on both his feet." II Sam. 9:13.

And this brings before us that most beautiful of all virtues, gratitude. "Gratitude is the fairest blossom which springs from the soul, and the heart of man knoweth none more fragrant," says Hosea Ballou. And concerning that terrible sin of ingratitude, Shakespeare makes King Lear to say, "How sharper than a serpent's tooth it is to have a thankless child."

For Jonathan's Sake. The friendship that had grown up between these two young men, David and Jonathan, was so deep that the Scriptures describe it in superlative language, "The soul of Jonathan was knit with the soul of David, and Jonathan loved him as his own soul." I Sam. 18:1. It is a classic among all writers to refer to the love of David and Jonathan whenever they wish to speak of surpassing affection and undying devotion of man to man. We need not recount here the many details of the common experiences of these two lovers, but we may perhaps state that at least once Jonathan was the means of saving David's life.

But Saul, the father of Jonathan, hated David, with a hatred as undying as was the love of Jonathan. So deeply had the canker of this David-hate seared its heated passion into the soul of Saul, that Saul became obsessed with a veritable demoniacal mania, that he must do no less than murder this young upstart of the house of Jesse. The terrible record reads,

"And it came to pass on the morrow, that the evil spirit from God came upon Saul, and he prophesied in the midst of the house: and David played with his hand, as at other times: and there was a javelin in Saul's hand. And Saul cast the javelin; for he said, 'I will smite David even to the wall with it.' And David avoided out of his presence twice." I Sam. 18:10, 11.

For Jonathan's Sake. And now years have gone by, and David sits upon the throne, and Saul is dead, and Jonathan is dead. Yet memory lingers, and memory brings back thoughts of other days. During one of those soul-searching reveries, David bethinks himself of those earlier years of his life, when every hour he was in danger, when he had to hide in caves, and behind huge boulders and beneath the webs of spiders, to elude the darts of the arrows from the bows of Saul and his henchmen. So we suppose one day there awoke in his heart the startling question, "What has become of Jonathan's family? Is there anyone left? I must show him kindness, *for Jonathan's sake!*" And so he sent out men to search through the kingdom to find if there should be even one scion of the house of the one he loved so dearly in those days of struggles and grief. And at last they came back. They had found one, and they brought him into the presence of the great king. And then King David did one of the most gracious acts of his life, he provided that Mephibosheth should eat at the king's table and should have every comfort and luxury as long as he lived. And then the Divine record tells us concerning Mephibosheth, "and he was lame on both his feet," which only means that he needed all the more the care and the attention of the servants who had been assigned to him by the King.

Him Whom They Have Pierced

For Jonathan's Sake. And now may we draw the application? Saul had actually thrown a javelin and had hoped to pierce the very heart of David. But Jonathan had befriended David, and yet Jonathan was Saul's son. And here we have Israel, who in similar vein did pierce the blessed side of our Lord Jesus Christ, and so in a comparative sense we may say that they thrust a javelin at One whose sitting upon the Throne they would do all in their power to prevent. Some day, as the prophet Zechariah tells us, this very nation shall "Look upon him whom they have pierced, and shall mourn for him as one mourneth for his only son." And the Revelator tells us in Rev. 1:7, "Behold he cometh with clouds; and every eye shall see him, *and they also which pierced him!*"

For Jonathan's Sake. Mephibosheth was lame on both feet. And lo and behold, in this present year of Grace, we behold the nation of Israel limping along upon two lame feet; there is that poor right foot of Orthodoxy, thoroughly infected with the arthritis of its own static "zeal for God, but not according to knowledge." And the circulation of the poor foot has stopped, and Orthodoxy has failed to function among the Jews of a new world and a new day. And then there is the other foot of Reformed Judaism, limping along and all but completely paralyzed by the cancer of their own

denial of the eternal verities of God's Word, so that it is
literally true as Isaiah laments, "From the sole of the foot
even unto the head there is no soundness but wounds and
bruises and putrifying sores." And so, Israel stumps along
upon these two feeble crutches, and of course we know that
a man with two crutches, with both feet lame, does not have
very much in his physical makeup to render him attractive
or handsome. But in spite of Mephibosheth's deformities,
David showed him kindness, "for Jonathan's sake." It is all
of grace, for he merited nothing at the hands of David; indeed if David were to take into account vindictively the
doings of Mephibosheth's ancestor, Saul, the normal desire
on David's part would have been to murder this grandson
on sight.

Here lies revealed the meaning of Romans 11:28, "beloved for the fathers' sake." We have here to consider the
integrity of God's oath. In II Sam. 21:7 we read, "The king
spared Mephibosheth...because of the Lord's oath that
was between them, between David and Jonathan, the son of
Saul." In the relation between David and Jonathan there is
the matter of the Lord's oath. No matter how ugly Mephibosheth might be, no matter how repulsive, no matter how
useless in life as a warrior or for any other service, he was
beloved to David, "for Jonathan's sake."

"Beloved for the fathers' sakes." In the annals of God's
dealing with mankind, only one human being stands out in
all the world's history, whom God called by the intimate
term, "my friend." That man is Abraham. What a marvelous,
unique relationship! To be singled out among all the races
of men, and to have God call him, "my friend Abraham,"
what wouldn't we give for such an honor?

And with Abraham God made astonishing covenants.
Malachi 3:6 gives us an insight into this profound situation,

for we read, "I am the Lord, I change not; therefore ye sons of Jacob are not consumed." In other words God tells us that the promises he made to Abraham and to Isaac and to Jacob concerning their seed forever, cannot be broken, because God by His very nature cannot lie. We call Him the unchangeable God, and in the New Testament revelation He is the same yesterday and today and forever.

For Jonathan's Sake. God is not blind to Israel's many sins. And we, too, have freely confessed the shortcomings of Israel; may the Lord forgive us if we have ever tried to deny the least charge of sin against Israel. But the difference between the Jew hater of the present generation and the true lover of Israel, the one who would follow God in these matters, is that the Jew hater loves to rake up the muck against the Jew and blazon it out with glee and malice, and to build out of this vile mess a campaign of ruin, desolation and extermination of the Jew from off the face of the earth. But God, when He presents the category of Israel's sins, invariably does it with tenderness, with love, and with the sure promise that He will restore them finally to His own favor, that He will freely pardon their sins, that He will bless them and make them a blessing to all the world. The one muck-raking is permeated with slander, hate and murder; the other indictment is saturated with love and fatherly affection. It is well for us to notice these earmarks of Jew-hating propaganda when we come across the satanic mouthings of those who on the surface suavely assure us that they certainly love the Jews, but they are only exposing the "apostate" Jews. Beware of this, for it is the kiss of Judas. As a matter of fact, all Jews are apostate Jews; we emphasize to our Jewish audiences over and over again that every Jew who does not believe on the Lord Jesus Christ is an apostate Jew, for he has rejected the supreme revelation of God's Word; so how can he be a real Jew?

The Tug At The Heart

And so, beloved friends, here is a new searchlight on the divine missionary teaching, "to the Jew first." The crippled child in the home somehow tugs the hardest at our heartstrings; and in the event of emergency, if the house catches fire, we run first to rescue the little one who is "lame on both feet." "To the Jew first," therefore, does not mean that the Jew is better than anyone else, it only means that he is in the more desperate need of our Gospel ministry.

And now we see the day approaching swiftly; the foretelling of Isa. 60:2, is unfolding itself before our eyes:

"Behold darkness (twilight) shall cover the earth and gross darkness (blackness of midnight) the peoples."

This is what the present world war means, this is what is slowly descending upon us as a black pall, the twilight of world civilization. Soon will come the inky blackness of such a midnight as the world has never known. Lights are out in Russia, lights have gone out in Germany, lights are out in Poland, and Rumania, and in many other countries of Europe. Most recently, to the shock of many, lights suddenly went out in Japan when a few weeks ago the war-mad leaders of that people told us to take back our missionaries! Soon will come gross darkness upon the earth, and then suddenly will come the miracle of Israel's rebirth, a nation born in a day, a nation that shall bow the knee to the Lord Jesus Christ, and surrender to Him their pride, their intellect, their entire national consecration. For we read in the second part of that same verse, Isa. 60:2:

"But the Lord shall arise upon thee, and his glory shall be

seen upon thee, and the nations shall come to thy light, and kings to the brightness of thy rising."

The Wisdom Of God

Do you not grasp the wisdom of God's program, "To the Jew first"? Year after year now for nearly fifty years, this has been the banner which we have nailed to the masthead of our Gospel ship, and year after year that little flag has stuck by the ship, in seas smooth and rough, and against waves small and great, against odds that many times seemed about to overwhelm us; but always we kept the flag nailed to the masthead, and our slogan, "To the Jew first," has never been lowered. We knew in our inmost soul that this was God's divine conviction to us, and we determined, with faces set like flint, to stand by the ship, whether it floats or sinks, but stand by we would. And God has honored us, and here we are today with forty-five years of faithful ministry on the records, and with a work more stupendous and more extensive than ever we dreamed God would allow us to see and to experience. And more and more He has given to us the friends and the fellow members of an ever enlarging family of those who love us and have stood by us these many years, with patience, with long-suffering, with the daily prayers of aching hearts, with rejoicing and thanksgiving when the Lord has given us special victories. These have been the great company of redeemed ones that we have loved to call our fellow laborers and our brethren and sisters in the Lord Jesus Christ.

And we are nearing Jordan, the brink of tremendous events about to be literally exploded upon a world rushing headlong into the greatest catastrophe of world history. The great event for which *we* look, is that blessed shout from the heavens; and together we shall labor for that lightning appearance that shall usher us suddenly into the bright light of His eternal presence. Until then, we shall continue in our humble service, both you and we as His workers together, doing that which He has committed us to do, giving the Gospel to all the world, but always "To the Jew first."

And this is what we have presented to our readers in some form or other, every January for a good many years past. And God has blessed these presentations, and those of His children who have been earnestly seeking to do His will have always rallied about us, and have told us plainly, "Go on with your work, we are behind you with our prayers, our warmest friendship, and our truest love in the Lord." And every January has witnessed unfailingly such an outpouring of gifts, "To the Jew first," that January has come to be the largest single month financially in our calendar. For many friends not only believe the doctrine, but they obey it literally, and they start the first month of the new year with the literal practice of giving the first missionary offering of the year, "To the Jew first." Our files are full of testimonies from some of the most devout of the Lord's people telling what blessings have come into their lives because of this practice. Your own Jewish Mission is also a first-class proof of this foundation policy. People wonder how it is that God has blessed this Mission in such an abounding way and has given it the privilege of witnessing the marvelous things that God has done for us. The answer is that we have fervently and sincerely sought to do God's work in God's way, and in that direction has lain the blessing and approval of God.

Beloved friends, what the year holds, only God knows; it may be that greatest of all years, for which all creation groaneth. But will you not pray that whatever the year has in store for each of us, we shall all be found faithful and so fulfill that which is required of a good servant?

THE BUTLER FORGOT!

January, 1943

Heartening and humbling are the letters of approval you keep sending us. How can we thank you enough? "A word spoken in due season, how good is it!" exclaims the wise Solomon in Proverbs 15:23. And our friends prefer to speak the good word to us now rather than to wait until the ears of clay can hear them no more, nor the heart any more quicken its beats to respond to the "God bless you, my brother." And so be it; for what is more fitting than that we should encourage each other as we together walk in the shadow of a rapidly approaching blackness which threatens soon to cover the whole earth?

So, once more a thank you in His Name. And we will lean still harder on the guiding hand of the Holy Spirit, to direct our every thought and word, for His glory, and for the edification of His saints. One brother writes, "Your paper is getting 'gooder and gooder' if that is possible." Another wrote, "The November 'Chosen People' is by far the finest you have ever put out." But we think we ought to say that it is only as He controls our thoughts can we even hope to be of blessing to you; and it is only as you keep praying so faithfully and earnestly that He will grant the answers. Little do people know, generally, what travail of soul goes into the getting out of each issue of this little messenger. But God knows, and we are so joyful that He honors His Word.

And now a new year is upon us. What it holds in prospect, no mortal can foretell. Truly the night is dark, and the night is also far spent. But the promise is, "The morning cometh!" Yes, the glorious morning of a Church caught up to be with her Lord forever. But, read on—"and also the night!" For after the bright morning of the Church's deliverance, there is going to be another night upon this doomed old world of ours, such a night of terror as never mortal saw before! But to us, who are His, there is the assured deliverance, and we walk by faith, and we say in full trust to Him, "One step enough for me."

To the keen watchful mind of the well-taught child of God, is it not becoming more crystal clear that the supreme task of the hour is to turn with a hitherto unknown intensity to the Lord's people, Israel? What else is the meaning of a world gone made with Jew-hate, but that God is calling to the Church as forcefully as any calling can be done, "Comfort ye my people!" What else is the meaning of ships bringing back to our harbors hosts of our choicest missionaries from all parts of a heathen world now insisting, "Away with your Christ!" Do not these facts of themselves constitute the clarion call to literally bombard a distracted and hysterical Israel with Gospel truth? And what means the fact that thousands of refugee Jews now in lands of exile, are uprooted from the old moorings, are shaken to their foundations, and, with hearts broken into tenderness, present to us the most fertile ground for Gospel seed that we have had in centuries?

The Butler Forgot

But we have forgotten! In our misunderstanding of God's program, we have made a program of our own. "The World for Christ!" has been the driving slogan of our "Kingdom" idea. And we have been hypnotized by the dream of world empire, ignoring the well-established Scripture fact that in this age God does not work that way; that it is the Holy Spirit which must do the outcalling, that we are only a feeble few who own His Name, that our incentive for world missions must be, not world conquest, but world testimony! That in that scheme of Gospel program, Israel must ever be held first in the thoughts of that Church. But we have forgotten.

And we think now of another one who forgot, in the long, long ago. He was a butler in the house of Pharaoh, and had been sent to prison for an offense against the king. There he was put in charge of that godly Israelite, Joseph, who, you remember, had been thrown into prison by the scheming and thwarted lusts of Potiphar's wife. The butler dreamed a dream, and in his great perplexity and even consternation, he turned to Joseph, the man of God, for light and comfort. And Joseph told him:

"Yet within three days shall Pharaoh lift up thine head, and restore thee unto thy place; and thou shalt deliver Pharaoh's cup into his hand, after the former manner when thou wast his butler. But think on me when it shall be well with thee and shew kindness, I pray thee, unto me, and make mention of me unto Pharaoh, and bring me out of this house: For indeed I was stolen away out of the land of the Hebrews; and here also have I done nothing that they should put me into the dungeon." Gen. 40:13-15.

When it shall be well with thee, show kindness, I pray thee, unto me! These were poor Joseph's parting words to a Gentile butler whom he had befriended. "Bring me out of this house," he begged. But tragic are the words of holy record:

"And he restored the chief butler unto his butlership again; and he gave the cup into Pharaoh's hand: . . . Yet did not the chief butler remember Joseph, *but forgat him.*" Gen. 40:21, 23.

The Butler Forgot! Shakespeare makes King Lear say of his cruel daughter, "How sharper than a serpent's tooth it is to have a thankless child!" And all through human experience, we have learned to place ingratitude at the head of the list of wickednesses. The Scripture does not say what blessings the butler lost because of his ingratitude, but we may be sure he must have paid many times the price for his faithlessness.

The Butler Forgot! Yes, but his forgetting did not thwart God's eternal purpose. God was at the helm, and He had determined that Joseph should be gotten out of the dungeon and be elevated to a position of power and blessing. The butler missed the glory, but God's purposes were accomplished just the same! It was the imperative business of the butler, the *very first* thing after his release from prison, to speak a word for Joseph; but he forgot! The Church may also forget to obey God's solemn command, "To the Jew First," but it is she who must suffer for it, and it is she who must lose the blessing. But God's purposes cannot be frustrated—He will find other means of bringing Joseph out of the dungeon!

The Butler Forgot! Do you see one Paul, imprisoned in Rome, awaiting a martyrdom such as we Christians of the modern age of comfort and ease know all too little? What is he saying? "Remember that ye being in time past Gentiles in the flesh!" Remember, that "He is our peace who hath made both one, and hath broken down the middle wall of partition between us!" Remember, "You are debtors to the Jews. For if the Gentiles have been made partakers of their (Israel's) spiritual things, their duty is also to minister unto them in carnal things." See Romans 15:27.

The Butler Forgot! What was the burden of Paul's life? Listen to words that should chill the very blood in your veins.

"For I could wish that myself were accursed from Christ

for my brethren, my kinsmen according to the flesh: Who are Israelites; to whom pertaineth the adoption, and the glory, and the covenants, and the giving of the law, and the service of God, and the promises." Romans 9:3-4.

Anathema from Christ? So deeply seared into the heart of this all-out missionary and apostle was this divinely revealed conviction as to the importance to God of Israel's salvation, that he would even have been willing to sacrifice his very eternity, if only it would bring Israel's conversion! *But the Church forgot!*

The Butler Forgot! Yes, brother, the Church has ignored God's program, and set up its own meager substitute. And what is the result? Apostasy! It is tragic to witness the evasions of our Church leaders when it comes to the question of the Jewish Mission. With the liberals, or so-called Modernists, the argument is "Let the Jews alone! They have a good religion of their own!" And every time they mouth these false words, they are confessing to bankruptcy in their own spiritual life, and to treachery to the Gospel which they have ostensibly espoused and from which they are getting their living. And in the same moment they are earning the contempt of the Jews themselves! So, they neither please God, nor do they win respect for themselves!

The Butler Forgot! But God did not forget, and after two long years He had given the butler the opportunity for what might have been the greatest blessing he ever would have experienced in all of his lifetime, God stepped into the picture and with His own mighty arm of deliverance, He brought Joseph out of the dungeon of despair and suffering, and elevated him to the place of world service, to the place where his far-sighted wisdom enabled him to bring deliverance and life itself to a land facing famine, starvation and death. And so we are going to see the same miracle repeated in the case of the larger Joseph as represented by the Israel of the world dispersion, and exile, and dungeon, and unspeakable suffering. When God in His marvelous patience will finally be satisfied that the Church, the butler who received from Paul that devout and heroic prisoner in the dungeons of Rome, the words of release, deliverance and salvation, He Himself will once more bare His mighty arm. He will take a little handful of Tribulation Jews and He will do a miracle in and through them. He will elevate them to the place of blessing, and it will be these Tribulation Jews that will go through a world of sin and shame and sorrow, and will make known the unspeakable riches of salvation through the Lord Jesus Christ! But alas and alack, the Church will have lost the blessing and the opportunity.

With the orthodox, or conservative, or Fundamental, group, we thank God there is a slow, but sure, dawning of light. Especially is this true where men have humbly and earnestly sought a fresh revelation of God's will for these days. More and more now, both churches, as well as individuals who are determined to be in His will, are obeying literally the order in Missions which God has established once and for all, "To the Jew first!" And in January, more offerings are made for our work than in any other month of the year.

Callous indeed, and hard-hearted, must be the one who, in this night of Israel's horror, can say glibly, "It is no more 'to the Jew first!' That happened a long time ago, but now it is over with. The Jew is no better than any one else!" But such a brother, strangely enough, fails to produce a single "Thus saith the Lord," to support or fortify his unscriptural fiat. And he further reveals his own animus in that he resents the putting of the Jew in any priority position in the cycle

of world-wide missions. But if God has done so, why should
such a one quarrel with Him? And the further truth, as we
have experienced it, is that when a Christian leader does per-
sist in his evasive "there is now no difference between Jew
and Gentile" you will find that the Jewish Mission has little,
or *no,* place in his own category of Gospel promulgation!
So, he contradicts himself, for he *has* made a difference, and
he has made it in favor of the Gentiles! Perhaps this may
be another reason why God said, "To the Jew first"; that, as
Paul put it, the Gentiles might not become "wise in your own
conceits!" So, perhaps the Lord established this rule also
as a disciplinary measure to Gentile believers. One thing we
do know, and that is, if this Mission of yours had not harped
persistently and relentlessly upon this fundamental missionary
doctrine, the Christian testimony and ministry to God's people
Israel would indeed be in a woeful and tragic state in this
America today! And who is there to say that we have not
been brought to the kingdom for just such an hour as this?

Satan Believes It

Strangely enough, the men who oppose and try to con-
tradict the once revealed truth and order with regard to
Gospel preaching—"To the Jew First"—do not seem to
realize that they are lending aid and comfort to the enemy
of our souls. For certainly it must be a striking thought, if
you have never given the matter attention, that Satan himself really believes in the doctrine of "To the Jew first."
Yes, the devil believes this, and together with Hitler, practices it! Only they do this *in reverse!* For has not the Jew
been always first in every explosion of world hate? Is it not
upon the Jew that the devil has ever concentrated his fiercest
fires? When the Pharaohs sought slave labor for the rearing
of their pyramids, "To the Jew first" was the passion which

possessed their wicked souls. "To the Jew first" likewise possessed the soul and body of such an arch fiend as Haman.

The World On Fire

As we write these lines, the shocking news comes of Japan's treacherous attack on our citizens and ships. And now, at last, we too are in the world holocaust. Our hearts are stirred, and out of the depths we can only cry out, "How long, oh Lord, how long?" And more than ever we need to comfort one another in the Lord; and more than ever must we intensify the Gospel testimony to Israel. In signs, in red lights, in signals so plain that they cannot be missed, God is fairly shouting at us, "To the Jew first!" And in the midst of these last dark hours of the world's Saturday night, we think of that beautiful picture of Malachi 3:16, 17:

"Then they that feared the Lord spake often one to another: and the Lord hearkened, and heard it, and a book of remembrance was written before him for them that feared the Lord, and that thought upon his name.... And they shall be mine, saith the Lord of hosts, in that day when I make up my jewels; and I will spare them, as a man spareth his own son that serveth him."

"They spake often one to another." It is the picture of the walk of children through a dark vale, a black tunnel, and fear of the unknown possesses each of us. It is then we reach for our fellow's hand, and we speak "often one to another" and so we go on the journey reassured and with new boldness.

May it be so even now among our precious family of "Chosen People" readers and ourselves here as your servants. And may this January mark the greatest demonstration of love for Israel your Mission has ever known! This must be the answer of every child of God to the neglect, the indifference, and even the sneer, the detractors of God's Book and of His people!

Our friends for the past year have placed at our disposal more funds than ever before in all our forty-seven years of labor; and, in order to be good stewards of these funds committed to our trust, we have promptly passed on the money over the seven seas, and to the four corners of the earth. Someone has called attention to the fact that the Lord loves a cheerful giver and he notes that the word cheerful really means hilarious. And so it is that God loves a hilarious giver; well, we have tried to match that giving by a literally hilarious dispatching of the funds to immediate service for the cause of the Lord Jesus Christ, and to bring quick relief into homes of distress and new hope to souls in the slough of despondency. All of which means that our friends have had the most efficient and effective administration of their funds, and we are grateful that God has used us in this way. But it also means that the Treasury starts the new year practically at the bottom of the barrel, and our lines must be laid for the coming year; we will plan the spending and the activities and the new undertakings upon the sheer basis of what God will indicate that we shall do when He moves upon the hearts of our dear family of friends in their responses to these enlarged opportunities and intensified calls. We thank God that He has given us far horizons and we want to stretch them even farther than ever before, in His good grace and mercy.

Every January we devote these first columns to a fresh presentation of the foundation missionary doctrine of your Mission—"To the Jew first." And every January we announce, "The Lord's treasury is now open to receive the gifts of His people for Israel's salvation." And every January our devoted friends literally pour in their gifts, their prayers, their affectionate loyalty. May it be so once more this January, for we now make the announcement, "The Lord's Treasury is open!"

We stand astride a world on the brink of destruction. To us come the S. O. S. calls by cable, by letter, by desperate personal appeals, "In God's name, help us!" We are ready to spend a million dollars this year for Israel the wide world over, if God gives it to us to do so; and every dollar will be spent efficiently, effectively, and to the abundant glory of the Christ we serve. Perhaps this is the last January we shall ever have on this earth! Who knows? Perhaps this is the year that shall be crowned with the shout from heaven, "Come up hither!" If so, then, "Come Lord Jesus come!" Amen and Amen.

TO THE CONSCIENCE OF AMERICA

January, 1944

"It shall be said of Jacob and of Israel, what hath God wrought!" Numbers 23:23.

For a good many years past our faithful friends have come to look to this January issue of THE CHOSEN PEOPLE for a fresh message of inspiration having to do especially with God's divinely ordained principle governing world wide missionary witnessing, "To the Jew First." Nothing needs to be said to the devoted army of believers who have cast in their lot with us these many years, who have entered with us into every experience in which our Lord has led us; they need no convincing, they have been convinced a long time ago that the only Scriptural method that God ever revealed to His Church for preaching the Gospel to the nations of the world, is "To the Jew First." That method has never been changed by God. And our friends have had this conviction burned deep in their hearts by the Holy Spirit; indeed such a conviction must come directly from the Holy Spirit's leading; because the natural heart, as witness what is going on in the world today, is filled with hatred for the Jew. And so these many friends have underpinned our labors, they have shed many a tear both of joy and of sorrow when they have read of the marvelous doings of God in our midst, of the persecutions, and of the miraculous victories achieved.

But even these friends love to have once in a while a little prodding or a little reinforcing to give them encouragement and inspiration as they go on, pilgrims together with us, ever moving forward on the road to the heavenly Jerusalem. And so we come now to a present day consideration of this missionary problem. I had thought to prepare for our readers a carefully reasoned out presentation of further Scripture teaching on this basic doctrine, but recent events in the world of nations, and their blood curdling cruelties against Jews, have rather abruptly and sharply brought into focus another angle of the problem which it might be highly desirable that our friends should examine. The approach in the present instance will be of a negative character, showing what has been the result of not obeying God's declared purposes with regard to Israel. You remember the poet's phrasing, "Of all sad words of tongue or pen, the saddest are these, it might have been." And then the Lord Jesus Christ voiced once perhaps the most tragic of all statements in the Holy Scriptures, when He told Israel, "If thou hadst known . . . the things which belong unto thy peace!" Luke 19:42.

A few days ago there appeared a startling advertisement occupying a full half page of the *New York Times.* It proved to be an appeal addressed "to the conscience of America." It was signed by the world famous author and journalist, *Pierre Van Paassen.* The advertisement began with a quotation of the first verse of that most beautiful of all passages in the Word of God, the 23rd Psalm, "The Lord is my shepherd, I shall not want. He maketh me to lie down in green pastures; he leadeth me beside the still waters." Then followed the most poignant and heartbreaking indictment of world civilization and American Christianity that ever our eyes have beheld. We quote a part of the advertisement that you may get an inkling of what this Dutch Jew is driving at; it is the pathetic unveiling of the heart of a disillusioned Jew. If the reading of these lines should bring you to your knees in more abundant prayer for Israel than ever before in all your Christian life, then our reprinting it in these columns will not have been in vain. The italics are ours:

"In that hallowed hour on Thanksgiving Day when President Roosevelt recited those words from the 23rd Psalm to the nation, seven thousand children of the people who first sang that Psalm were led out of the ghetto of Warsaw to be slaughtered.

"The day before and the day before that, the day thereafter and the day after that, the same harrowing thing occurred: more thousands of Jews were massacred. For Hitler is not merely boasting that the Europe he has conquered will be made *Judenrein,* he is feverishly at work translating into reality his threats to exterminate the Jewish people root and branch wherever they may be found.

"To the Jew of Europe the green pastures have become a big ditch he is forced to dig with his own hands before falling into it riddled by volleys of shots from the Gestapo's execution squads. The still waters are pools, nay, a rising river of blood . . .

"Day in, day out, the torment goes on. The details of the massacres are almost too hideous to be put into words. They are appalling. Nothing so bestially cruel has been recorded in the annals of history.

"Air bubbles are injected into the veins of tens of thousands of Jews, resulting in agonizing death in a short time. . . . Men, women, and children are pressed into airtight chambers where they are choked to death en masse with poison gas. . . . Elsewhere, as in Vilna, Jews are herded into disused slaughterhouses and done to death by electric currents that pass through the specially installed metal flooring on which they stand. Jewish mothers have been compelled to look on as German soldiers played football with babes and newly born infants . . .

"Did Dante in his awful vision see anything as gruesome in hell?

"Every day our State Department's figures reveal a larger number of Jews slain than the British people lost in the entire year 1940, the worst year of the air blitz. The Jews have nearly two million victims to mourn, and each hour the mountain of their martyred dead rises to still ghastlier heights . . .

"When, a quarter century ago, the Armenian people were subjected to systematic spoliation and murder, the Christian world cried out its indignation and protest. When the stream-lined barbarians of our day leveled Rotterdam to the ground and buried 30,000 Netherlanders under the ruins, humanity's heart stood still and sickened. When they burned Lidice, a cry of horror went up from the civilized world.

"The Jew has seen a hundred Rotterdams. He has witnessed and experienced the horrors of a thousand Lidices. Every step he takes in Europe is stained with his own blood. Yet, no action was undertaken to stop this ruthless process of annihilation. There has not been an official word of protest or indignation in America following the State Department's recent harrowing revelations—not a word of rebuke or disgust, of shame or warning.

"Hardly a word from the Christian churches! Not a word from governmental authorities! Not an adequate word from the moulders of public opinion in the press and on the radio! Not a word from the intellectuals, the guardians of civilization!

"That silence, sinister in its implications, has now lengthened into weeks. And Jews are still being slaughtered.

"Are we so callous or so inured to calamity and horror that we cannot take notice of an old people's anguish or hear the death-rattle in the throats of millions of human beings?

"Are the United Nations so weak, or so cowed and intimidated by Hitler's bloody face, that they do not even dare to talk back?

"Dr. Goebbels, the Nazi Minister of Popular Enlightenment, wrote not long ago in his weekly newspaper *Das Reich*: 'if the day should ever come when we (Nazis) must go, if some day we are compelled to leave the scene of history, we will slam the door so hard that the universe will shake and mankind will stand back in stupefaction!'

"Now, having seen the writing on the wall in the unbroken fighting spirit of the Red Army and in America's ability to wage offensive war on both sides of the world simultaneously, the butchers of Berlin have begun to slam the door. They have started to do to the Jewish people that fiendish thing which is to cause the human race to reel back aghast, just as every act of barbarism and every piece of inhumanity they ever perpetrated was first tried out on the Jews.

"What the Nazis are doing to the Jewish people today is a foreshadowing, a foretaste of what is in store for all the peoples in the occupied countries. It is the beginning of a program of terror and horror that is ultimately to be applied to Poles and Czechs, to Dutchmen and Yugoslavs, Greeks and Frenchmen.

"At the time when the Nazis came to power and singled out the Jews for their first attacks, *the democracies stood aside, invoking the political doctrine that there must be no interference in or notice taken of the purely internal affairs of a foreign state.* Moral considerations had to make way for the rules of the imperialist game of blood and guile when great nations like the Czechs and the Austrians were to be handed over to the sadists of the Reich. We distrusted reports about the inhuman treatment meted out to Jews in the murder camps of Dachau and Oranienburg. We shrugged our shoulders as if it was no concern of ours what Streicher and Himmler did to a few thousand German citizens of the Jewish faith.

"We were yet to learn, at an immense cost in tears and blood, that humanity is one, even as God is One, and that the martyred Jews were merely the forerunners on the road of sorrows of Poles and Albanians, of Czechs and Norwegians—and of American mothers and fathers.

"We were yet to learn that the anti-Semitic justification of the Hitlerite's attitude to the Jews was but a trick to lull the Christian nations to sleep, to divide the democracies, to obscure the issues at stake, to befuddle people's minds in order that they might fall victim the easier to the Nazi plans of world conquest.

"To be silent in this hour when thousands of unarmed, innocent Jewish human beings are murdered each day is not only a betrayal of elementary human solidarity, it is tantamount to giving the bloodthirsty Gestapo carte blanche to continue and speed its ghastly program of extermination.

"To be silent is to help Hitler carry out his program of killing off one people today—another people, perhaps the Poles, tomorrow, and the Czechs and Yugoslavs the day after tomorrow, when the American Army proceeds to the offensive against the European continent, and Hitler, in desperation and fury, will seek to remove the danger of uprisings in his back.

"Our present silence is growing audible in Berlin. For us to say that we will do our best to find a solution for the Jewish question after the war is a mockery, and only evokes laughter in hell. At the present rate of killing, there will be no Jewish question left to solve . . .

"Let America speak out!"

The immediate purpose of the advertisement was to crystallize sentiment to persuade Great Britain to allow the Jews to form a separate Jewish Army in Palestine. We are not here endorsing such a proposal, nor is this the time or place to discuss the merits of the idea. Personally we find ourselves out of sympathy with the plan, but that is not the purpose for which we reprint this stirring advertisement. We see, and we hope our friends likewise will see with us, a mighty and a transcendental force in this powerful indictment, and one which leads directly down the road to the thing that we have been talking about not only in the beginning of this letter, but for the forty-eight years of our existence. It is the inevitable but evil result of disobeying God's fundamental command with regard to the Jew, a disobedience in which the nations as such and the organization called Christendom as such, have both been inexcusably guilty.

Niemoller's Terrible Mistake

"Hardly a word from the Christian Churches!" What a scar such a charge must make upon the sensitive conscience of the real child of God within the organization of Christendom! Can you see once more the poor bleeding victim who had been stripped of all his possessions, and was lying wounded, half dead? The priest came that way, but when he saw him he passed by on the other side. Likewise a Levite came and looked on him, and passed by on the other side. And then came deliverance at the hands of a Samaritan, who had compassion on him.

What has the Church been doing? While Israel has lain bleeding and over two million Jews have been slaughtered in Poland alone by the wicked hands of the Nazis, the Church of Christ is busy "reconstructing the social order," and some of their misguided leaders are running up and down the country holding conferences to discuss what kind of a peace they are going to make with Germany! And forever over the doorway of time God has laid down the order to the Church, "To the Jew first!" What a terrible accounting some of these leaders will have to give in that day of judgment! Just look a moment at what happened in Germany: Niemoller, representing, at least in symbol, the Christian testimony of Germany, actually played along with Hitler during the first four years of the Jew-hating campaign of the Nazis; he did it of course in all innocence, and he says now that he thought that the Nazi hate for the Jew was only a passing fancy, and would stop as soon as Hitler was sure of his power. But poor Niemoller woke up four years too late, to find that the fangs of the demon serpent of Jew-hate had reached down into his own church and was destroying its very vitals until now there is no church in Germany! If Niemoller and the Christian church in Germany had stood steadfast upon the rock foundation which God gave two thousand years ago, "To the Jew first," they could have defied Hitler, they could have told him to keep out of the churches, to leave the Jew alone; in that hour the church was strong enough in Germany to have wrung Hitler's neck. But no, the church was lulled into a false sense of security, and before she knew it, Hitler's bestial foot was upon her neck; and all because the Church failed to obey the instruction "To the Jew first."

Nations Equally Guilty

"The democracies turned aside!" This indictment is reminiscent of God's bitter denunciation against Edom, in Obadiah:—"In the day that thou stoodest on the other side, in the day that the strangers carried away captive his forces ... *thou wast as one of them!"* And so these world nations

have proven false to their trust. Among all nations, God has scattered the Jews, and by doing that He has definitely created a trust for which these Gentile nations must give an account. It is Israel whom God has cast upon the seas of the world nations, and Israel is the testing ground of these nations. True, God has been displeased with Israel and God has been punishing Israel for these two thousand years, but that was not the business of the Nations. Just read again the incisive indictment that God gives on this point, Zech. 1:15, "I am very sore displeased with the nations that are at ease; for I was but a little displeased (with Israel) and they (the nations) helped forward the affliction!"

We like to idealize our wars; in fact, it is only by idealizing them that we can gain national morale and national acclaim. That is the function of all propaganda machinery of Government. But such idealizing should rather be called rationalizing, because it is a noteworthy historic fact that no nation goes to war for an ideal, or for a humanitarian principle. They go to war because they have been attacked and they must preserve their national existence; they go to war for aggrandizement, for territory, for greed; but after the war has started then they fall back upon some ideology so as to give their people the enthusiasm needed to keep up the morale for winning the war. We mention this because we want to stress the everlasting fact that no nation goes to war for humanity's sake; otherwise we are face to face with a devastating contradiction—if Great Britain and America and France ten years ago, when first the demoniacal hand of Hitler fell with such a thud upon a helpless body of Jews, and they were being slaughtered and treated in such ways as to make civilized brains reel and shudder, if in that hour, these three nations of the world, Britain, France and America, would have united and told Hitler, "This butchery and savagery against the Jews in your country must stop! If not, we will invade your country and blow you to pieces!" If these countries had done that, it is one of the surest things that there would now be no world war and no Hitler; for what was true of the church in Germany, was also true of these world nations. For, in the very infancy of Hitler's rise to brute power, these world nations had the ability to stop him on twenty-four hours' notice! But no, what did they care? A few thousand Jews to be butchered, more or less, made no dent on their conscience; after all it was "an internal affair of the German government." And so the conscience was lulled to sleep, and today the nations have Hitler. All because they failed to stand by the Jews in the hour of anguish.

How Long Shall We Remain Blind?

Need anything more be said? Will any sane reader question the conclusions and the indictments that we have now perforce had to make in these columns? Are there still those among Christian people who are callous enough to deny to the Jew his God-given place in the missionary program of the Church? Can you not see more clearly than ever before the eternal and infinite wisdom of God in having laid down this principle for the church to follow? We are well aware that many well intentioned Christian people, both pastors and laymen, fight bitterly when they hear us present the claims of God with regard to Israel. One such pastor was quite vociferous in talking with me not long ago about this matter. "I differ with you radically," he told me, "in your claims about the Gospel being given to the Jew first. I believe it is for everybody in equal order, and that the Jew has no prior place, but should be given the Gospel the same as everybody else." He seemed to be holding his temper with great difficulty, and I sensed beneath the surface an almost implacable resentment against this established teaching of God's Book. So when he was finished I said to him, "Very well, supposing for a moment that we assume that your position is correct, may I ask how much money your church gave this year for Jewish missions? You have just told me that you think the Jew should have the Gospel just the same as other people, and now I want to know how much you gave for Jewish Missions this year; did you give to the Jewish work just as you did to other Missions?" His face got red, and he was silent; I pressed the question however, and finally he had to admit that his church had not given a single dollar for the cause of evangelizing the Jews! And so, the cat was out of the bag, and I trust he saw to his own shame what the consequences are when one starts out to deny God's Word and to say that the Jew is to have the Gospel like anybody else. We have discovered so many times that such a claim is only an evasion, and results almost invariably in the Jew receiving nothing from the church. Is this not also another powerful explanation why God gave the commandment, "To the Jew first"?

The Lord's Treasury Is Open

And so with this sad background, we do once more what we have done these many years past in January; we open the books of our Treasury for a new year, and we say to our beloved people, "The treasury is open, the Lord invites you to make such an outpouring of your gifts in this the first month of the year, and thus literally to the Jew first, as you have never done before." This is the hour of challenge, this is the hour when on every side the Jew is suffering such anguish as never known before in history; even your own Jewish Mission would be extinguished tomorrow if only the enemies of the Jews had their way. Our friends have known this for many years, and they have always answered the challenge by laying down sacrificially such heroic gifts that the enemies have marvelled and have been stunned to see how this Mission has plowed through the waves of distress and persecution, with God on the bridge deck; and He will remain as our Pilot, until in that last blessed day He shall bring us to that haven which is the desire of all those that go down to the sea in ships. The promise is, "So he bringeth them unto their desired haven." Psalm 107 : 30.

Somehow we hope and believe that we shall have the largest January, financially, in our history; for it has become increasingly the blessed custom of our people to set aside their gifts until the month of January, and then to release them for the Lord's work in our hands. You will rejoice to know that we are closing last year as the greatest year since first my dear father opened the little store in one of the thorofares of that section of Brooklyn known as Brownsville. Our own hearts have been not only astonished, but cheered and encouraged to go on with ever larger ventures for Him; because, behind us have been the cheers, the prayers, the tears of those whom we have learned to call our friends, beloved friends, and true friends.

And now may the New Year bring to each one of our readers a peace and quiet such as the world cannot give, in the midst of its own din; above all, we have the blessed assurance, "Behold I come quickly," and from the depths of our hearts we voice the response that came from the burdened heart of the seer of Patmos, "Even so, come Lord Jesus!"

"LIFE FROM THE DEAD"
January, 1945

" 'To the Jew first' is a marching order which we have neglected."

So says Bishop Fulham of London, England, in one of his recent pronouncements having to do with the failure of the Church of Christ to carry out the commission which the Lord Jesus Christ Himself gave to her. Bishop Fulham continues,

"The golden age of evangelism was when a handful of converted Jews in obedience to their Lord's command went forth and proclaimed Christ as the Saviour of all mankind. Let us ask ourselves whether the slowness of the progress we are making may not be due to our neglect to use to the full what I believe to be a real power-house of evangelistic effort. I have confirmed and ordained Jewish converts and have found that the old Apostolic zeal is there and they yearn to bring others to know that Mr. Jocz is right when he says: 'Unfortunately the Christian Church as a whole has shamefully neglected its duty towards the Jews and the Christian Mission to Jews is still treated as a step-child of the Church. It is still the most unpopular and the most misunderstood enterprise amongst Christian people !' "

And no less an Anglican than Bishop Worcester of England, came out the other day with a startling manifesto to the Christian world. He said that he had decided just for an experiment to read the New Testament all over again as though this were his first reading, as though he had never before seen the book and was now approaching the revelation afresh. He said that to his astonishment he found himself in a sort of panic; for it came to him with the revelation of a lightning storm, that above all else the New Testament rings through and through with the one teaching that the Gospel must be given *to the Jew first!* The Bishop of Worcester frankly confesses that the failure of the Church to obey this elementary principle in world-wide missions has been the real cause for the calamities that have come upon the world and for the failure of the Church, which now has reached a point of staggering apostasy.

We mention these things now because for a good many years past we have made it a habit to devote these January pages to a repeated presentation of the blessed truth which so many of our people have learned to love, to believe, and to practice, that is, the giving of the Jew the same primacy as to Gospel preaching that God has given him in His blessed book, *to the Jew first.*

Say It Again And Again

And we have found that no matter how profoundly and fervently our dear friends believe and practice this blessed revelation, they always rejoice to have it discussed and rehearsed. It is just like the man who has been saved, and rejoices ceaselessly in telling of his salvation. And we always try to bring some little fresh light on the subject, so that you will be strengthened and cheered and blessed as you contemplate afresh the increasingly strategic importance of this age-old teaching in the Word of God. The other day a pastor in one of the large churches in the southland, said to one of our friends, "Mrs. .... is a member of my church, and is one of the wealthiest women that we have; but on the first day of every January, the first check that she writes out, is made to the American Board of Missions to the Jews up in New York City; she has done this for years, and for the life of me I have done everything that I could think of, but cannot stop her from doing this!" And so here we have rather the seamy side of the question; and it does seem a pity that a Christian pastor instead of rejoicing that the dear woman is obeying God literally, year after year, is disturbed about it, and is doing his best to stop her!

I have thought that on this occasion, when the world situation is reaching the point of catastrophe, and Israel is looming to the front as never before since the destruction under Titus, we should consider what others, apart from ourselves, are thinking and saying about the relation of the Church to Israel. For God is in these last days opening the eyes of some of His choicest servants to see this long-neglected necessity of putting the Jew first in the category of the activities of the Church.

One of the most beloved and helpful little books that came out of the 1941 crucible of God's dealings with His own, is a little book entitled, "Sirs—Be Of Good Cheer." The writer is none other than Mrs. Howard Taylor, the daughter-in-law of the sainted J. Hudson Taylor whose heart and life burned out for his beloved China. And although Hudson Taylor gave his life for China, and believed with an enthusiasm born of God, in the missionary undertaking among the Chinese as well as other heathen nations, yet this is the Hudson Taylor who on the first day of every January, year after year, as long as he lived, made out his first check of the new year, to his friend, John Wilkinson of the Mildmay Mission to the Jews of London, England, and always marked the check, "to the Jew first!"

We would reasonably expect that the mantle of such a saint of God should have fallen to his son or, by proxy, to the son's wife. And it is even so, because in the very center of the book, is a chapter, "Our Strongest Plea," in which is presented such a moving cry for Israel as we have rarely seen or heard even from the greatest advocates of Jewish Missions. Here are a few pages:

"When the heart is wrung with the world's great anguish, when we feel our own utter helplessness, do let us fall back upon very definite as well as urgent prayer. But what are we to pray for? How shall we order our petitions according to the will of God? Is not that just our weakness, that in the confusion of world happenings we do not know what to pray for as we ought?

"Since this is so can we do better than make use, as David did, of God's own purposes and promises to guide us? Psalm 67 is like a great searchlight turned upon the suffering world, then and now, at once locating the trouble and showing the remedy:

" 'God be merciful unto us (Israel), and bless us, and cause his face to shine upon us, that thy way may be known upon earth, thy saving health among all nations.'

"Read it, ponder it, follow its guidance, for there is authority behind it, the authority of a divine covenant that bears upon the world situation today. And what is this covenant between God and man, this divine promise that cannot be broken? It is rooted back in great, unchangeable facts, sealed with blood and confirmed by the most solemn oath:

" 'By myself have I sworn, saith the Lord, for because thou hast done this thing, and has not withheld thy son, thine only son, that in blessing I will bless thee ... and in thy seed shall all the nations of the earth be blessed; because thou hast obeyed my voice.' Gen. 22:16-18.

"There it stands, immutable as God Himself. Heaven and earth may pass away, but His word never can, till all be fulfilled. The blessing, then, of this world is to come through the seed of Abraham. Oh, that the eleventh chapter of Romans might take its right place in our thinking, and therefore praying! Humanity is like a body out of joint. Something is wrong with the world—what can be plainer? And Scripture tells us that only when Israel is restored to its true position, by the mercy of God, can the body of which it is so vital a part function properly. Individuals can be and are saved through faith in Christ, though the Chosen Nation is estranged through unbelief; but a restored and readjusted Israel is to be God's channel of blessing to a redeemed world. For the covenant still stands: 'In thy seed shall all the families of the earth be blessed.' (Acts 3:25 R. V.)

"How full, then, of meaning is the prayer, 'Have respect unto the covenant, for the dark places of the earth are full of the habitations of cruelty.' Let us get back to real foundations; and this, surely, is one of the most stable. What is the condition of Israel today? And what is the condition of the world? Do we bewail 'the dark places of the earth'? Then why neglect the surest way to put right the grievous wrongs that cause our hearts to bleed? Israel must be uplifted, transformed, restored; for Israel, too, is redeemed by the precious blood of Christ. Was it not a Jew who was inspired to write of His infinite sacrifice as 'not for our sins only, but also for the sins of the whole world'? Are we earnestly praying for the turning of the Jewish people in faith to their Messiah? Are we giving, working in every way open to us, for their deliverance and enlightenment? Do we see the essential connection between their present sufferings and the rising tide of the world's misery? Never, until the Jews are restored to their own land and to the heart of God, can earth's wrongs be finally put right and suffering humanity healed.

" 'For if the casting away of them be the reconciling of the world, what shall the receiving of them be but life from the dead.' Rom. 11:15.

"And, thank God, the time has come for this restoration. Nothing can be plainer from the prophetic Scriptures than that the long day of Israel's rejection on account of their departure from God is drawing to a close. And what follows? Does not the inspired Word thrill our hearts—'Thou, O Lord . . . shalt arise and have mercy on Zion: for the time to favour her, yea, the set time is come.' (Psalm 102:13).

" 'Have respect unto the covenant,' the covenant with Abraham and his seed for ever. What a plea to put into our lips! Are we making full use of it? This is 'the day of Jacob's trouble.' Amid all the sufferings of this sin-stricken world there is no darker page than the wrongs and woes of Israel today. 'But he shall be saved out of it,' is God's own word (Jer. 30:7). As we read and re-read the four chapters that form the charter of deliverance (Jer. 30 - 33) the great question stands out, 'Is there anything too hard for the Lord?' God asks it, and God answers it in that magnificent passage, linking with His purposes the prayers of His people:

" 'Call unto me and I will answer thee, and show thee great and mighty things (fenced in and difficult) which thou knowest not.' "

Need anything more be said? When a dear servant of God whose heart is bound up in China will write a book on the foreign mission question, and make the very heart of the book a burning plea that the Church shall wake up and understand the place which God has for the Jews both now and in the world to come, surely it is time for the easy-going Christian in America to stop short and give serious pause.

In Bibliotheca Sacra of May, 1942, appears a review of this book of Mrs. Taylor's. Here again we have a slant from perfectly impartial sources, which surely ought to convince the most skeptical and the most hardened of hearts. We are quoting just one or two paragraphs from that review:

"This is one of the most excellent of books, verily a soul-thrilling volume, and supremely adapted to these troublous and anguishing days.... The heart of the book is in chapter VII. 'Oh that the eleventh chapter of Romans might take its right place in thinking and therefore praying. Humanity is out of joint. Something is wrong with the world—what can be plainer? And Scripture tells us that only when Israel is restored to its true position, by the mercy of God, can the body of which it is so vital a part function properly.'"

"Never has the reviewer had anything come to his heart with greater spiritual uplift and thrill. Only the Word is superior."

In another magazine, there appears a most interesting story directly on the subject we are now considering, and we are giving it herewith as follows:

"A story is told of those true friends of missions, both to Jews and Gentiles—Charles Simeon and Edward Bickersteth —to this effect: They were once present at a meeting held in support of the London Society for Promoting Christianity among the Jews. Simeon was the speaker, and in closing his speech, he said that they had met together that day for the furtherance of the most important object in the world, viz., the conversion of the Jews. When Simeon sat down, Edward Bickersteth, who was at that time a secretary of the Church Missionary Society, wrote on a slip of paper, 'Eight million Jews, eight hundred million heathen—which of these is the more important'? This paper he handed to Mr. Simeon, who at once turned it over and wrote on the other side: 'Yes, but if the eight million Jews are to be as "life from the dead" to the eight hundred million heathen, what then?' And this done, he returned the slip of paper to Mr. Bickersteth."

We have said enough on these matters, and we must stop now because our space is so limited. We do just want to repeat what we have said on many other Januarys, that once more the Lord's treasury is open to receive such an out-pouring of the gifts of His people for a greater ministry to Israel than ever before we have known, that will break every record that ever a January has produced before, and will say to us in no uncertain tones, "We are with you heart and soul, dear brother, go forward, and like Ruth of old wherever thou goest, we too will go." Knowing the generosity and the warm-heartedness of our dear people through the years gone by, we can rest our case at this point, and go right on with our work knowing that from across this country, from the west and from the east, from the north and from the south, will come the hosts of the Lord to our help. And we will take up again the gauntlet of the Gospel challenge, and press on to ever-newer heights of victory for Him.

What a morning there is going to be when the Sun of Israel's righteousness shall shine forth with the brightness of noonday brilliance, and the nations of the world shall learn war no more, but shall go up to Jerusalem and from Jerusalem learn how to serve the true God!

For The New Year—God Be With You

And now to our own beloved friends; may we add a few wistful words in your behalf? There is not an easy year ahead for any child of God; heartaches there are and there will be without number; the world war may be over sooner than we think, perhaps before you receive these very lines.

On the other hand, this war may continue until it becomes literally a holocaust, and until nations shall be clutching at each others' throats and reel back only when they are utterly exhausted and bled white. Whatever the future holds, may we all learn the blessed truth of the promise, "My times are in thy hands." No matter what happens, the vacant chair in the home, the boy raving in delirium in some army hospital, the father's heart torn to pieces with the agony of just thinking. Through it all we must, as His born-again child, hang on tightly to the blessed assurance of Romans 8:28, and we must say to ourselves over and over again, "He doeth all things well." What goes on now, we may not know and we may not understand, but we have the absolute promise that there is going to come a time when we shall know and we shall understand. And He Who has called us and sanctified us, and sealed us for His Body, the Church, will see us through to the end, and not one of us will ever slip through His fingers.

And so may the coming year, whatever it may have in store by way of historic events, nevertheless bring to each one of us a new experience in God's faithfulness, and a new trust in His eternal purposes.

VOICES OF THE PAST

January, 1946

"Peace be both to thee, and peace be to thine house, and peace be unto all that thou hast." 1st Sam. 25:6.

This is the greeting out of our hearts on the occasion of the New Year, and this is our earnest prayer for every one of our dear friends, both far and near. Some of the eyes that read these lines now may be dimmed by tears; into some hearts there may have come the full measure of sorrow and grief; but to all such may the blessed greeting from the lips of the Saviour Himself "Peace be unto you!" come with fresh power, dispelling all clouds and causing sorrow and sighing to flee away! True it is that such counsel as this may be easy to give; but beloved brethren and sisters, we speak earnestly out of our heart, and what we say to you we have said to ourselves many and many a time. We have taken our own medicine first before we have passed it on to others. The truth is that as born again children of the living God we simply have to abandon all our hopes, our possessions, our expectations, to the sure guarantees of Romans 8:28— *all things.* And we testify gladly that the remedy has proven effective and valid with us, so that we can say in words of II Cor. 1:4:

"Who comforteth us in all our tribulations, that we may be able to comfort them which are in any trouble, by the comfort wherewith we ourselves are comforted of God."

What an anchor to our souls it is to realize that in the midst of a changing world, with cataclysms staring us in the face, destruction on every side, that we have the God of Jacob for our refuge, and that our destinies are linked, not with this earth, but with Him Who holds all things in His power and with Whom we are foreordained to reign forever and ever. So thus we are only pilgrims passing through this vale of tears on the way to the everlasting heritage of that eternal city, the new Jerusalem, where every shadow shall flee away, and time shall fade out into endless eternities.

The First Month—The First Gift

The first month of the year brings to the front once more the age old and divinely ordained plan of God for world wide Missions—"To the Jew first." Year after year you have sort of expected us to bring your hearts and minds a fresh emphasis of this most vital of all missionary truths. So many of our most devoted fellow laborers just look forward for January to come, to bring them the privilege of their heart's desire, to make their first offering in the first month of the year, literally "To the Jew first."

This Jewish question will not down; we cannot evade it. And this is true in every sphere of human activity, whether it be on the battle field, in world economics, in intellectual leadership, or in the very heart of the missionary undertakings of the Church of Christ. No one with even half an eye open, can fail to see in the present world convulsions, God's majestic stride as He shifts and shuffles the confused forces of world powers so as to bring to the attention of these blood-crazed nations the Jewish problem. Like Wisdom, in Solomon's exhortations, the Jewish problem is crying out, it cries in the chief places of concourse, in the gateways, in the streets, everywhere where the streams of men pass by, to all who will hear, to all who will not hear.

But men hate this missionary doctrine, "To the Jew first." It runs counter to their pride, to their conceit, to their own carnally concocted schemes for world Utopias. Even in so-called orthodox circles, this primary obligation of the Church for whom our blessed Lord gave His life, is too many times ignored, or set aside deliberately, or even held in contempt. We have ourselves been sneered at, ridiculed, mercilessly attacked, all because we have dared to hold this basic truth in the structure which God has so carefully blueprinted in His Word for the upbuilding of His Church. Sometimes we have felt like a lone voice crying in the wilderness, like the owl of the desert, of which the Psalmist speaks, and as a sparrow alone upon the housetop. But always the Lord has been our defense, our tower of strength, and we have experienced over and over again that just one, if he has God with him, makes the majority. Years ago the Lord gave to us a promise to which we have clung like the drowning man to his raft, and which, praise God, has been our bulwark through every storm that has come, never failing us, always protecting us, and always lifting up a standard for us against the enemy. It is Isaiah 54:17, "No weapon formed against thee shall prosper." The storms have come, and the angry waves have dashed their fury against us, throughout these fifty years of rugged history. But always that protective promise, "No weapon formed against thee shall prosper" has proven to be the voice of our Saviour rebuking the angry waves, and telling them with supreme authority, "Be still!"

It Is Woven In The Fabric

Like the blood stream running through the river of God's redemptive program for this world, and emptying itself out at the towering Cross, on Calvary's Hill, so the missionary doctrine, "To the Jew first," courses its way through the entire fabric of God's missionary pattern for the Church during her parenthesis history. Ye must, ye must, and again, ye *must* be born again, is the inescapable *sine qua non* that God has declared to this world of men. There is no other way. It is the inescapable imperative, *"ye must be born again!"* And just as surely as this divine truth runs through the declarations God has given to His Church to shout to the world of sinners, so truly is there an inner pattern that governs the *method* by which the Church is to do her declaring; and that inner pattern shouts just as loudly, just as understandably, ye must, ye must, and again ye must, go "to the Jew first!"

Whether we like it or not, whether we believe it or not, the bald truth is that there is in the world a devil. The race of men which is now fast approaching that tragic hour when iniquity will have come to its full, hates this devastating fact. The pride of life, the conceit of philosophic sophistries, the exaltation of the ego, these tragedies combine in a formidable host which does not hesitate to throw blasphemously its defiance against God Almighty and His revealed purposes. A devil there is; otherwise how explain a Hitler, a Goebbels, or even a Stalin? Think of the idiotic vaporings of a Satanically blinded leader of the blind, who a few days ago audaciously declared in a so-called "religious" broadcast on the radio, that there is no evil in the world! What we call evil, this blinded deceiver declared, is only Good in reverse! Imagine the thousands of people listening in on such a broadcast of drivel!

But the point is that if God has commanded His Church to give the Gospel "To the Jew first," it is Satan's business to do his utmost to make the Word of God of none effect. It is the story of the ages, for Satan is still asking, and this time from the very church leaders who are supposed to be earnest in their serving of the Lord Jesus Christ, "Hath

God said?" We have learned that whenever a devout child of God begins to cavil at this God-given command, or begins to twist the passages, or to sidestep the issue in any way whatsoever, it is only Satan at work; so we just ignore it, and wait patiently for the time to come when God will give the brother such an awakening that everyone of his dry bones will shake as did the dry bones of the vision of Ezekiel.

Voices Of The Past

Adelaide Proctor, in her beautiful poem with the above caption, paints a wistful picture as she tries to show that it is to the past that our hopes and memories are to be anchored:

> O there are Voices of the Past,
>   Links of a broken chain,
> Wings that can bear me back to Times
>   Which cannot come again:
> Yet God forbid that I should lose
>   The echoes that remain!

Through a most acceptable coincidence, our beloved young brother, Dr. Charles L. Feinberg, came across some reports published in 1888, of the Centenary Conference on the Protestant Missions of the World, held in Exeter Hall, London, in that year. As we dipped into those records, we could not help bowing in at least a gesture of respect to the great men that gathered in those days to discuss the things which belong to the Lord's kingdom. Because back in those early years God did stir the hearts of some of those spiritual giants to see the awful sin of the Church in her neglect of the Israel to Whom God is eternally committed. We wondered if these voices of the past might not be an inspiration to our modern generation of helter skelter, catch as catch can, opportunists. Cried Jeremiah of old, "Ask for the old paths, where is the good way, and walk therein, and ye shall find rest for your souls!" Jer. 6:16. Surely this generation needs to go back to the old paths.

The Question Of The Ages

For so in some of the discussions of the London Conference, we came across some striking and even impassioned pleas, that the Church shall rouse herself from her indifference to a vigorous and militant espousing of the cause of Jewish missions, so that such missions shall have a place in the very front lines of the battle for the souls of men. Here are some of the stirring appeals that were made at those sessions; we have condensed them drastically to make room for as many as possible:

JAMES E. MATHIESON, Esq. I remember, beloved friends, that at the great Missionary Conference held ten years ago at Mildmay, the only reference to the work of God amongst His ancient people was confined to a portion of the closing meeting. The whole Conference had been passed over without any reference whatever to Jewish Mission work. I recollect that on that occasion my heart burned within me with a good deal of indignation that this matter had been put into such a distant corner of the Conference program, and I uttered a word or two from Psalm 67, which distinctly intimates to us that the blessing of the world is to come through the greater blessing descending upon God's ancient and beloved people. My dear friend, Dr. Schwartz, who has been taken home long ago and gone to see the King, used to say, "You Gentile Christians take all the sweet promises of God to Israel for yourselves, but you leave all the curses to the poor Jews!"

In our great ecclesiastical gatherings the last verses of

Psalm 122: "Pray for the peace of Jerusalem; they shall prosper that love thee. Peace be within thy walls, and prosperity within thy palaces," etc. But they do not mean Jerusalem, and they do not mean the Jews; they mean the Established Church and the Free Church of Scotland. Is not this something like "robbery for burnt offerings"?

REV. JOHN DUNLOP. About seventy years ago, Dr. McCaul published "The Old Paths" in which he exploded the errors of the Talmud, and unfolded the truth in Christ. This book has been useful to many a Jewish inquirer, and lately to a cultured and venerable Rabbi, named Lichtenstein, who lives in a quiet place called Tapio-Szele, near Buda-Pesth, in Hungary. Rabbi Lichtenstein read the book, and then resolved to answer it. He sat down to write a paper in order to defend the Talmud, and if possible to degrade the teaching of the Christ; but he rose from the task a changed man. Since then he has been led to call the Gospel of Christ, "That sweet evangel." He has published three remarkable pamphlets, addressed to his brethren throughout all lands, in which he calls them to believe in the Lord Jesus Christ as the Messiah of Israel, and the Saviour of the world. (Editor's note: This is the world famous Rabbi Lichtenstein who ultimately took his synagogue out from the other synagogues of Buda-pesth, in a bold espousal of the cause of Jesus Christ as Son of God and Israel's Messiah. Rabbi Lichtenstein was a hero of the faith, of such a sort, that one cannot read his life without realizing he is face to face once more with a chapter in the Book of the Acts. It is the grandson of this famous Rabbi, Emanuel Lichtenstein, who is now our missionary in the Argentine.)

Jewish Missions had no place at all in the Conference at Nuremberg, until Dr. Delitzsch, at the very last moment, in a spirit of astonishment, sorrow, and reproof, rose, and in burning language, reminded the assembly of the great omission and Israel's transcendent claims. This meeting to-night demonstrates that we have made some progress since then. Jewish Missions have not only a place here, but a first place; and yet we must express our regret that an entire week should be devoted to Gentile Missions and only three hours given to the subject of Jewish Missions, which the Holy Ghost, through Paul, teaches us are of supreme importance. Listen: "For if the casting away of *them* be the reconciling of the world, what shall the receiving of *them* be, but life from the dead?"

REV. JOHN WILKINSON. (Founder of the Mildmay Mission to the Jews.) My purpose is to direct the thought, prayer, and effort of the Church of Christ to the line of the Divine plan; since the power placed at the disposal of the Church—and that is amazing power—is available only on the line of plan, so the fullest blessing lies along the line of obedience to Him we call Lord.

Is it true, or is it not, that God's power lies along the line of plan, and that God's blessing is the result of obedience? If true, let us ascertain the plan, work along it, and wield the power; and let us search out the commands of our Lord, yield obedience, and get the blessing. God's promise to Abraham was, "I will bless thee," "I will bless them that bless thee," "and thou shalt be a blessing" and "in thee and in thy seed shall all the families of the earth be blessed." And our Lord said, "Salvation is of the Jews." God says by Isaiah, "This people have I formed for Myself; they shall show forth My praise."

"To the Jew first," is still in force as a matter of order, not of pre-eminence. These were the last instructions of our risen Lord, and should be carefully noted.

The Church of Christ has changed this order. And why? We suggest that when Jerusalem was destroyed by Titus in the year A. D. 70, when the temple, sacrifices, and priesthood were all swept away, and the Jews scattered, the Christians began to regard the Jews as done with, rejected of God spiritually as well as nationally, and that they might first neglect them and then persecute them.

Obedience to the Divine order was followed by marvelous blessing to Jews and Gentiles; a reversal of the order in disobedience to God was followed by the dark ages and very limited blessing.

The Church of Christ seems to have no idea of the loss she sustains from lack of interest in Israel. *It is not at all improbable that the secondary cause for closing this dispensation in corruption and judgment, on the completion of the Church and the return of the Lord, will be the culpable neglect of the Jew by the Church of Christ.* Let us, then, be obedient to our Lord, and go, "first to the Jew," and we shall find the line of plan, the line of power, the line of obedience, and the line of blessing. "Whatsoever He saith unto you, do it."

REV. H. SUMMERBELL, D. D. I love the children of Abraham. I have now preached for fifty years, and all through my ministry I have had friendship shown me by Jews, and I believe that some have died in the faith of the Lord Jesus Christ just because they were brought to think seriously about Christianity by my loving them and they loving me. All our Scriptures were Jewish Scriptures; our Lord's Prayer was said to the Jews first; our dear Saviour was born of the Jews, as far as the flesh is concerned; our religion comes from the Jews; the first churches were composed of Jews; the first fourteen Bishops of Jerusalem were all Jews. We trace our religion, not back to Rome, but above

Rome, up to Jerusalem. The first history of the Church is the Acts of the Apostles, and it is a history of Jewish preachers, Jewish churches and Jewish councils.

Oh, let us pray for the Jews! The Jews have suffered more persecution from the Christians than the Christians have suffered from all the pagan nations together. The reason why the Christians turned so violently against the Jews after the destruction of Jerusalem was that the Jews were disgraced and destroyed, a great portion of them murdered, five hundred of them hanging on crosses at once before Jerusalem, and many thousands made galley slaves. It was a disgrace to be called a Jew. The Gentile Christians ignored them. They made a fatal mistake. Pray for the children of Abraham!

REV. ABRAHAM HERSCHELL. You must remember that this is a dispensation of an election from among all nations. I read in that pamphlet of Mr. Johnston's that whilst there were three million converted during this century, there were two million of heathen and Mohammedans added each year to the population that need conversion. As if it were a new revelation! It was not new to me, for this had always been my understanding based on Scripture. I hear people talking of Mission work as if it would be converting all the nations, as if the nations were standing still, and did not propagate and progress in population. I should have been very much discouraged if I did not believe that God does not intend in this dispensation to convert nations as nations, but that He intends that the Gospel should be preached as a witness, and a people gathered out for His praise and glory from all the corners of the earth. I have never been discouraged, because I take the Scriptural view of the state of things. This is the dispensation also for the gathering out of God's people for God's praise from the people of Israel. Nothing more. National conversion will take place by and by when the Lord Himself shall appear. Now you have not realized the fact that the gathering out of the remnant according to the election of grace is quite as great among the Jews as it is among Gentiles. And in reality when one considers what small efforts have been made, one is perfectly astonished how in every part of the world God has His elect among Israel. I remember asking Dr. Moffat when he came back from Africa and was a member of my congregation, "Did you come across any Jews in Africa?" "Well," he said, "I came across three Jewish converts from St. Helena." Just think, from St. Helena! One, Saul Solomon, he said, became a very eminent man in the legislative assemblies of the Cape; two others became ministers, and had large congregations.

REV. PRINCIPAL DAVID BROWN, D. D. (Distinguished theologian of Aberdeen, and co-author of the famous commentary on the Bible prepared by Jamieson, Fausset and Brown, 1864-70). I may remark that from the time I first began to study my Bible experimentally—shall I tell you how long since that is? It is seventy years ago—I felt that as salvation is of the Jews, and my own Saviour was Himself a Jew, and He is God over all, blessed for evermore, I felt drawn to the Jews by ties which have become stronger from that hour to this. Every word that has been uttered tonight about beginning with the Jews, beginning at Jerusalem, to the Jew first, I not only echo, but I practice it. One word more. How many of you every Saturday morning, and perhaps on Friday evening, pray for Israel when they come to keep the Sabbath day? How many of you make a business of it to cry aloud for the Jews? I suppose in England that not one in a thousand makes any special prayer for the Jews at any special time, and I think that is a great pity.

And so, beloved friends, here we have a cloud of witnesses. Need more be said? One cannot but be profoundly humbled as he stands in the presence of these blessed voices of the past. It is as though these men had actually arisen out of their graves, and with burning passion, were beating at the doors which guard the citadels of our hearts, begging us almost in the words of Paul himself, "I beseech you therefore, brethren, by the mercies of God that you present your bodies a living sacrifice." And again, "As though God did beseech you by saying: we pray you in Christ's stead, be ye reconciled to God." II Cor. 5:20. And, dear brother and sister, this business of being reconciled to God has to do not only with the forgiveness of sins but also with the necessity of being reconciled to Him in the doing of what He has told us to do as regards His people Israel.

And this is the rock on which your beloved Jewish Mission has been built, and God has honored it these many years; He has planted it, He has watered it, He has allowed it to bring forth blessed fruit for Him. And somehow we believe that He is grooming this Mission of yours for the greatest opportunities ahead, of all of our history. What vistas of Gospel privileges open up to us as we try to peer beyond the immediate mist of the world wars, to that other day when countless millions of wandering Israelites will reach out desperate hands of appeal to us, crying out, "Come over and help us!" To that end the Lord has been graciously replenishing our treasury so that we shall have funds immediately the war stops, that will allow us to proceed without delay in pouring out the succor that will be so agonizingly needed in that pregnant hour.

The large denominational Boards are engrossed in the raising of huge funds for their Post-war "reconstruction programs." They speak ignorantly, but volubly and plausibly, of the "better world in the making!" seemingly not knowing or caring that God's sword and sickle are being made ready for the harvest and swift judgment. The Methodists are raising the enormous sum of $25,000,000, and the other denominations in proportion. Shall not the Jewish Mission have consideration? And shall the children of Light be outwitted by those who are strangers to God's revealed counsels and mysteries? Is a million dollars for a Jewish Mission Post-War Fund a thing too hard with God? Or too staggering to our faith? Or too much for the envy of those who seek our hurt?

The Lord's treasury is open again the first month of the new year to receive a new outpouring of His People so that in the Lord's house there shall be plenty and in abundance for use against the day of want. The individual friends, each beloved by us as a member of our precious family, and the increasing number of churches, all of whom have been led of God to turn their steps in our direction, and to say to us, "Where thou goest, I will go"; all these are as the springs and the rivulets that start forth from their mountain heights to bring the waters of refreshment to the great rivers and lakes and oceans of the world; these rivulets course their way to our Mission Treasury, to form a reservoir out from which will be poured lifegiving waters to the souls that shall be in thirst and in want in the calamitous days that are surely on their way to this earth. It is the old dream of Pharaoh which Joseph was given divine wisdom to explain; seven fat years there were to be, years of prosperity; then just as surely, there were to follow seven years of leanness, and famine and desperate want. So we too must prepare as Joseph did of old for the years of want that are ahead, and for those days when tribulation shall begin upon this earth and the Jewish testimony will perhaps suffer. For above all things, God must and will always have His witness and His testimony upon the earth. And we in the present generation are instruments in His hand for the carrying out of His eternal and stupendous purposes.

IT BEGAN WITH THE JEWS

January, 1947

A blessed chapter was written into this "anthology" of "To the Jew First" upon the occasion of the dedication of the LEOPOLD COHN MEMORIAL BUILDING in New York, when a friend of the founder of the American Board of Missions to the Jews, namely, Dr. Hugh R. Monro, presiding at the exercises, paid a tribute to Leopold Cohn. Dr. Monro is one of the outstanding Christian laymen of America, an elder in the First Presbyterian Church of Orange, New Jersey, and a leader whose counsel is eagerly sought, and highly esteemed, not only in Presbyterian denominational circles, but in practically every evangelical undertaking in this huge Metropolitan area. A director or officer in more than twenty businesses and leading religious enterprises, one cannot but marvel at observing his seemingly endless energy and his tireless and aggressive labors in the Lord's service; and with it all a modesty that utterly disarms anyone who has the privilege of having fellowship with him. With quiet strength and assured confidence in the Lord Himself, this giant among God's noblemen gives forth his own original convictions out of the Word of God through his personal and profound study of the Book—and does it all without fear or favor.

Dr. Monro is the last link still surviving from the days when Dr. Leopold Cohn, back in 1894, began knocking wistfully upon the doors of Jewish homes, and at the hearts of Christians, seeking, lone voice in the wilderness, to make known the saving Gospel of the Lord Jesus Christ to his brethren in the flesh; and seeking also, as a stranger in a strange land, to find among people who were followers of the

Lord Jesus Christ, a friend here and a friend there who would say to him, "Go on, brother, I am with you, I will help you, I will pray for you, I will fellowship with you."

Such a friend Dr. Hugh R. Monro proved to be; but with the passing of years those other precious friends having gone on to be with the Lord are now a cloud of witnesses. They died in faith, not having received the promises, but having seen them afar off. Only one remains—Hugh R. Monro. To him we turned, in making plans for Dedication Week, to inquire whether he would like to preside at the Dedication Memorial night service. In spite of the burdens he is carrying, and a bodily health that is not what it used to be thirty or forty years ago, this godly man said, "Yes," he would come in from Montclair and be with us to take part in the Memorial.

His address that evening was a memorable one. He began by describing his first meeting with my father, followed by a profound presentation of how the Gospel first began, back in the Book of Acts, to be handed over to the Gentiles by Jewish Christians. He told first of his early connections with Leopold Cohn, and of the almost unbelievable sufferings that had been undergone by this pioneer man of God. He told of actual and brutal physical beatings, of the most shameful experiences of defamation of character by men who called themselves Christians; of envyings, of jealousies, of every known scheme of Satan to destroy the testimony of my father's work. He said that the example of this hero of the faith had been a means of great blessing and encouragement to him. With the deepest spiritual emotion that was felt on every side and that pervaded the entire Chapel hall, the meeting was dismissed. There were many tearful faces and many ejaculations of, "Thank God," and some people told us that they will never forget the experiences of that night. So we thank God ourselves, and we try to express at least a little bit of our thanks to Dr. Monro.

Another distinguished guest was Dr. W. H. Rogers of the First Baptist Church of El Paso, Texas. Dr. Rogers had formerly been the pastor of the First Baptist Church here in New York, made famous through the ministry of Dr. I. M. Haldeman. Therefore, when Dr. Rogers was announced on our own program, many of his friends and admirers gathered to greet him again. Perhaps the best thing that we can do is to quote a few sentences from his first address:

"I count it a great honor to be associated with this Mission and to share in the fellowship of this high hour and auspicious occasion. It has been my joy to be connected with this work for many years. I knew its founder, Rev. Leopold Cohn, and my associations with him have filled my mind and life with many sacred memories. He suffered for his faith, and if I were to put what I knew of his life into a single sentence, I would say he was a silent sufferer for God and his faith. I have great veneration for his memory, his devotion to Christ and the truth, and this Mission, which is the heritage he has passed on to us. Somehow I feel his spirit very near at this dedicatory service, and in loving memory of his life and works we dedicate this Mission to God and all the things that He held near and dear. We do not gather here to pay him any glory, he would not have it so. We do, however, pay this tribute of love to his memory and dedicate this spacious building to the God of Israel and to God's Christ and His Church.

"There is a scene of Old Testament times that this meeting recreates for me. It is found in 1 Chronicles 28:20: 'And David said to Solomon his son, "Be strong and of good courage, and do it: fear not, nor be dismayed: for the Lord God, even my God, will be with thee; he will not fail thee, nor forsake thee, until thou hast finished all the work for the service of the house of the Lord." '

"You will pardon me if I paraphrase this to read in this manner: 'And Leopold said to Joseph, his son, "Be strong and of good courage, and do it." ' Surely the mantle of the father has fallen upon the son, and there is no one that would be more overjoyed upon this occasion than Joseph's father. The growth and expansion of the Mission are the fruits of the combined labors of father and son and their associates of the years, among whom has been our honorable Chairman, Dr. Hugh R. Monro. I congratulate the General Secretary and the Board upon the wisdom they have demonstrated in securing this building, which is in such an excellent location for the doing of the work we have in mind. I feel confident that the kind of glory that is upon us now will be upon the Mission in the years to come, and many an Israelite will be saved through the Gospel that will be proclaimed in this building we dedicate to God.

"A brief outline of the message I would like to bring you can be put into three sentences:

"First, our debt to Israel, which can only be paid in our obedience to Christ by giving the Gospel 'to the Jew first' and also to the Greek.

"Secondly, God is with and for the man who labors earnestly to give his precious Word to his ancient people, Israel.

"Thirdly, Satan is opposed to that same man and the kind of work he is anxious to do.

"This gathering carries my mind back to words of 2 Chronicles 6:12, 17: 'And he stood before the altar of the

Lord in the presence of all the congregation of Israel and spread forth his hands.' We stand at a similar altar making our vows to the Lord in the presence of His people. 'Now, then, O Lord God of Israel, let Thy Word be verified which Thou hast spoken unto Thy servant, David.' That same Word will be verified by the faithful exposition of God's Word. It will be verified in the exaltation of Christ, for which this Mission is reputed. It will be verified by the testimonies of transformed souls who will have been brought into a saving knowledge of our Lord and Saviour, Jesus Christ. It will be verified by the outreach of that same Gospel from this center to the uttermost parts of the earth.

"We commend all the associates of this Mission to the Grace of God and pray that we may be true to the principles and faith of the man, its founder, whose name will be a cherished memory as long as life shall last for us."

Dr. Charles H. Stevens of the Salem Baptist Church in Winston-Salem, N. C., was another loyal friend of the Mission who took a prominent part in the program. He had brought with him a beautiful chart that stretched almost across the entire wall of the Chapel hall, and from that chart he taught both Jews and Christians the foundation truths of the span of God's grace through the ages. All were deeply impressed, and we are counting on Dr. Stevens' coming back to us at a later time for a longer ministry.

Another friend, our good brother, Dr. Thomas Lawrence, came in from Yonkers and took part with us by giving a devotional address. We are counting on him to help us later on in further Bible-teaching work here. It is becoming more and more evident that our New York Headquarters is to be a Bible-teaching center for prophetic truth, whereby we shall reach both Jew and Gentile through one unified ministry.

Another fearless voice was that of Rev. J. Murdock Palmer, President of the New York Baptist Ministers' Association, who told us of his high appraisal of the testimony and work of this Gospel Mission to the Jews.

Our brother, Hall Dautel, having come to us all the way from Erie, Pa., gave us much encouraging assurance of his fellowship with, and his love, for us. May the Lord bless him in his faithful ministry of the Word at Erie.

Dr. H. McAllister Griffiths, General Secretary of the American Council of Christian Churches, brought a message concerning the Jew, the Gentile, and the Church, that made many of us do some fresh thinking.

From The Pacific Coast

What can we say of Dr. L. Sale-Harrison, who has proved himself to be a brother with heart as closely knit to us as was the heart of Jonathan to David? He was so determined to be with us, and had such a deep-rooted love for the Mission, that he sent us a telegram from Tacoma, Washington, that he was changing all his plans in order to be here for the Dedication Week. And what a glory he gave to the Week! He could not speak in terms strong enough to tell of his love for the Mission and of the unquestionable privilege and duty of every child of God to stand by the work, to pray for it, to fellowship with it.

As usual, our Dr. Charles Feinberg captivated the audiences with his searching exposition of the Word. He presented the Prophet Zechariah for the entire week, and the people who listened daily thanked God for the new light received. Dr. Arthur I. Brown also came to rejoice with us and gave us a stirring message on "The Eleventh Hour."

So the week closed. It took us a number of weeks to get our breath again, and to begin to lay the foundation for the new work, and the meeting of new problems with new methods. We know that He is with us, and our only dependence will be upon Him. We are now launched and count on your prayers and faithful standing by until we shall see the glory of God manifested here in ways that we have never known before.

God's Order Still Stands

Here it is January, and once more it is our blessed privilege to present, albeit briefly this time, a dissertation on the foundation rock upon which this Mission was built, the categorical imperative of Romans 1:16, "To the Jew first," and the age-old divinely ordained program for Missions. We believe in our very hearts that our friends will surely and faithfully follow these instructions of our Lord, without a fresh urging. It is however, a distressing symptom of these times that there are men who are servants of the Lord Jesus Christ, but who actually hate the teaching of God's Book that the Gospel must be given to the Jew first. Can this be one of the signs of the end-time, that Satan is using these very servants of God, to be unwitting tools in his hands for Jew hate and for deliberate violation of God's command? As one dear brother wrote to us, "What is there to question or to hesitate about? The Book says, 'To the Jew first'; I have no choice but to obey what God has told me to do."

A strange phenomenon came to our attention not long ago, showing how vacillating even some of the best-informed of Christian men can be. A certain Bible study publication came out in its November, 1943, issue with an article entitled, "To the Jew First." We print it here verbatim:

"There can be no longer any doubt that we are seeing the days of Israel's restoration in unbelief, and that He Who is not only the Hope of Israel, but first of all the hope of the Church, is very near, even at the door. Yet a little while and He that shall come will come and not tarry. But in the little while of His tarrying it is our blessed duty and privilege to witness for Him, and that means *at the end of the age the same as it was in the beginning of this dispensation, to the Jew first.* (Italics ours). That this is the divine plan is made clear by the open door the Lord has given among His brethren according to the flesh. Oh, you who love His appearing, you who love Israel, pray for the peace of Jerusalem, give Him no rest till He establish and make Jerusalem a praise in the earth. Continue to scatter the New Testament and Christian literature among your Jewish acquaintances. It is a seed sown in hope; it is blest of God and will bring a glorious harvest."

But lo and behold, this same paper in the issue of June, 1945, printed in a question and answer column the following item:

"*Question:* Is it not true that we should preach the Gospel to the Jew first, and then to the Gentiles, in accord with Romans 1:16?

Answer: God's chosen people, Israel, should always be upon our hearts, and we should reach them with the Gospel of our Lord Jesus Christ as well, as promptly, and as widely as possible. But Romans 1:16 does not refer to the order of our preaching the Gospel, but to the order in which it *was* proclaimed. (Italics ours). The early Jew had the Law. He had the Temple with its divinely instituted worship. When Messiah came He came first to His own people. After Christ's death and resurrection and after Pentecost, repentance toward God and remission of sins were preached to the Jews first, by Peter, before he had the vision of the sheet. Paul, although a chosen vessel to bear the Name of the Lord before the Gentiles, preached first to the Jews. All the apostles were told to be witnesses first to Jerusalem. But the

Jewish people who rejected Messiah in the first place refused, as a nation, to hear and heed. However, to them the Gospel of Christ was first proclaimed, that Gospel, "Which is the power of God unto salvation, to the Jew first, and also to the Gentile."

Apparently something must have happened between these two issues. We cannot help but think of the challenge of 1 Kings 18:21, "How long halt ye between two opinions?"

The Answer To Satan's Machinations

So may we not say that we do trust confidently that this January our friends will not only do what they have done in January of past years, that is, set aside their first gifts in the first month of the year literally "to the Jew first," but that there shall be such a super-generous outpouring of these gifts that it shall take its place as the largest month financially in all of our history. This shall be the answer, sweeping and conclusive, to the specious wiles of those well-meaning persons, who are being used, perhaps without their knowledge, as Satan's pawns in the strategic battle of wits between God's unimpeachable instructions, and Satan's unceasing defiance of those instructions. The Lord's people have the answer to all this in their own hands, and they can administer needed rebukes to misguided leaders any time they choose to exercise such power. The closing hours of this age are forging Israel's destiny in God's eternal purposes in such a way as to make it almost criminal for any child of God to put one straw in the way of carrying them out.

The Lord bless you out of Zion, and the Lord make this year to each one of us a year in which our fellowship with Him will reach greater depths of love and devotion, and blessed communion, than ever we have known before.

HAS THE CHURCH ROBBED THE JEWS?
January, 1948

In one of his orations, Cicero said, "The rabble estimate few things according to their real value, most things according to their prejudices." It is amazing to witness from time to time the extent to which prejudice can blind the one who allows it to become his master. We suppose that life is full of the tragedies brought about by the blunders of sheer prejudice. It was Whittier who gave us an immortal reminder of lost opportunities when he wrote in Maud Muller:

> For of all sad words of tongue or pen,
> The saddest are these, "It might have been!"

If only we had done this, or if we had done that, instead of the things that we did do! If only we had not allowed our prejudices to blind us, what a different story we might have to tell!

We Encourage Each Other

All of this is by way of prelude to this New Year's greeting to all of our precious family, a greeting in which year after year, in January, we present a dissertation on the foundation upon which the American Board of Missions to the Jews has been established; and that is God's divine order in Missions, "To the Jew first." Thanks be to God, an ever-increasing host of His most devoted children have gathered about us and strengthened our hands in support of this tragically neglected truth of God's revelation; and even these friends seem to be grateful if from time to time we give them fresh encouragement and new light, as God may give it to us, upon this basic principle in world-wide missions.

Malachi tells us, "They that feared the Lord spake often one to another."

It was our good friend and brother, Dr. W. H. Rogers, formerly pastor of the First Baptist Church of New York and now pastor of the First Baptist Church of El Paso, Texas, who when he was with us at our Summer's End Conference last August, made this searching indictment of certain ones—both preachers and laymen—who had allowed their prejudices to turn them against Jewish missions: "When a preacher or a layman tells you that he rejects the Bible teaching 'to the Jew first' but believes that the Jew should have the same place in the world missionary program of the Church as the Gentile, what he means is that he does not give anything at all for Jewish missions!" We, ourselves, have found this to be true in a wide experience covering many years of travel over our country. Almost invariably the church which rejects the Bible teaching "to the Jew first," ends up with giving the Jew nothing at all! Thus, the true inward meaning of their prejudices becomes apparent.

The Guns Are Loaded

With the alarming rise of Jew-hate that is threatening America as a tidal wave; with the coming into existence within recent months of new organizations that have sprung up like mushrooms in various parts of the country, whose publicly-announced object is to destroy the Jews; it is indeed a tragedy to think that this Jew-hate may seep into the churches of our land, and find no wall of resistance nor any forces of combat against the inroads of this Satanic propaganda. If such should reach into the vitals of the Christian Church, then surely the climactic hour of world disaster will have come, and God Himself will have to write Ichabod across the pages of a Church that has surrendered to this most subtle and devastating of Satanic strategies.

Indeed, is not the present blindness to the need of Gospel ministry to the Jews on the part of so many of our orthodox churches, the greatest weakness and even the greatest sin of these churches? Many years ago I listened as a student to the enticing descriptions of a glorious millennium for the Jews, when once they had been returned to the land of Palestine and had been restored to God's favor. The teacher was none other than the now sainted Dr. James M. Gray of the Moody Bible Institute. He painted a glowing picture of Israel's glory which would come to its fruition in some far-distant day, the time of which had not yet been revealed. We can still remember Dr. Gray making a most gracious bow as he said by way of comment on this vivid portrayal of Edenic bliss for the Jews, "Every time I see a Jew I feel like taking my hat off to him."

Israel Needs Salvation Now

Not a word was said about the Jew needing salvation right here and now. Nothing was said about the tragic fact that a Jew who dies in his sins now without the redeeming blood of the Lord Jesus Christ, is just as much lost as is any Gentile who dies without Christ. I could not help but wonder whether, if the future glory of the Jew was to be so marvelous, I had made a mistake, and should not have become a Christian! So I went to this great saint of God personally, and asked him point-blank, "Have I made a mistake in becoming a Christian? If the Jew is to have such a wonderful future, shouldn't I have remained a Jew?" For a little while the great Bible teacher was nonplussed; he looked at me long and hard, and I realized that he was facing a situation and a question that he had never thought of before. Finally he said to me, "No, my boy, when you are in the Church of Christ, you are in the highest calling in all creation, a calling far above that which the Jews nationally will enjoy here on the earth in the millennium." Then I said to him, "If that is true, why do you not tell it to your audiences? And why do you not encourage the Jewish mission testimony, and do all in your power to win Jews to Christ?" It was my joy some years later to read a pronouncement given out by Dr. Gray in which he said that after years of Bible study he had come to the conclusion that the Church of Christ surely owes the Gospel "To the Jew first." So Dr. Gray, after a long life of service for the Lord, came to see that this keystone in the arch of world missions had been shamefully neglected by the Church.

Words Are Not Enough

All through the years we felt it as an inescapable duty to shout from the very housetops the call for consistent Christian practice on the part of these men who were making such ado about the people of Israel (one might almost say they were exploiting the Jews!), and yet at the same time they were not even lifting a finger to help to bring them the message of salvation through the Lord Jesus Christ which, after all, is the only hope of Jew and Gentile. We have been pleading and begging these brethren to be consistent; that they shall do more than merely say sentimentally, "Every time I see a Jew I want to take off my hat to him." No greater blunder was ever made by some of these "premillennial" teachers than when they propounded the unscriptural idea that this is the time when God is gathering out a Gentile Church. There is no such thing in all the Scriptures. Such a claim is a libel on God Himself and should be rebuked whenever it raises its head. The only Church spoken of in the Word of God is, THE CHURCH, where both Jew and Gentile sit together in heavenly places in Christ Jesus, both rejoicing in the same salvation, in the same Saviour. It would break your heart if you were to follow the tortuous story of how trusted leaders in Christendom have dishonored the Word of God by evading and twisting it when they came to the Jewish question, or indeed to anything with Jewish flavor. How many millions of Jews have been kept out of the Church through the centuries because of this unfortunate twisting, only eternity will reveal; and how great must be the responsibility of those who followed such twisted policies, will also be revealed in that day when the hearts of men shall be laid bare before Him, the Judge of all nations.

The 144,000 Tribulation Jews

In line with the policy we have followed since this Mission was established, we prepared a special advertisement several years ago entitled, "Who Will Preach the Gospel When the Church is Gone?" For the sake of the record, and to prepare you for what is to follow, we reproduce the advertisement herewith:

WHO WILL PREACH THE GOSPEL WHEN THE CHURCH IS GONE?

If you are a well-taught child of God, you know the answer—the Jews, of course. We call them sometimes The Tribulation Jews. To them we must hand down our Torch of witness, that they may carry on, after we have heard the shout from heaven!

And if this is true, then do you not see the categorical imperative involved? It means that the true Church must now evangelize Israel with a fervor and intensity never known before, to prepare that Remnant to take up the Testimony once the day of Grace is ended. This is the deeper meaning of the Jewish mission witness, and we are not asleep when it comes to an understanding of the inner workings and necessities of God's dispensational program.

In 1945, Dr. Oswald T. Allis, formerly in the Department of Semitic Philology at Princeton Theological Seminary, editor of the *Princeton Theological Review* and Professor in Old Testament Department of Westminster Theological Seminary, wrote a book entitled, "Prophecy and the Church," in which he exposed some of these very errors on the part of certain Christian leaders, and showed with lucid incisiveness the inconsistencies of their position. Of course, we cannot agree with all that Dr. Allis has written in his book, and much of it can be shown to be based on fallacious understanding of what God is doing in the present age. But one does not have to swallow the errors of a book in order to benefit by some of its constructive teaching.

"For They Say, And Do Not"

Dr. Allis quotes the advertisement mentioned above, and then he accuses us of being party to the errors of some of these premillennial teachers. But what he failed to understand was that all we were doing was to take the basic teachings of these well-meaning teachers, and compel them to face the logical imperatives of their position; in other words, our sole purpose was to say to these brethren, "It is not sufficient just to say a few pretty things about the Jews, you must also be consistent in what you say, and fulfill your unquestioned obligation, by following out the implications of your professions." Of the Pharisees the Lord bitterly complained, "For they say and do not." All that we are asking is that these brethren shall not be guilty of the same conduct.

But Dr. Allis goes a great deal further as he exposes the inconsistencies of these brethren who through some mistaken conception of the purpose for which the age of the Church was brought into existence, would strip the Jew of all his rights not only in the Abrahamic covenant, but of his ordinary prerogatives as a human being, as well. Dr. Allis' exposé is all the more sensational and all the more effective, because he writes, not as a premillennarian, but as one taking a contrary position. We are not sure whether Dr. Allis would classify himself as a post-millennarian, or as an a-millennarian; but it is with searching rebuke that he opens up on the weaknesses and inconsistencies of some who call themselves premillennarian. Especially apropos are the paragraphs under the heading, "Robbing Israel," in which he turns the tables fairly and squarely against their pre-judged (prejudiced) fatalism as they seek to side-step the inexorable demands of the Word of God in the matter of winning Jews to Christ. We quote one or two of these paragraphs:

"Since Dispensationalists are so insistent that Christians have 'robbed' Israel of promises which are peculiarly and exclusively hers, by interpreting the Old Testament kingdom promises as applying to, and fulfilled in, the Christian Church, it may be well to consider this question somewhat more fully. We have already admitted that this accusation finds justification and support in the attitude of Christians towards the Jew in the course of the nineteen 'Christian' centuries since Pentecost. The Church has not only appropriated the blessings to herself and pointedly applied to the Jew the curses which the prophets uttered regarding Israel; but what is far worse, she has often by sins of commission and of omission excluded the Jew from the Christian Church in which she professes to believe these promised blessings are exclusively to be found. The early Christians were instructed, in their proclamation of the gospel, to begin at Jerusalem. Both Peter and Paul began with the Jew. But the Christian Church has for centuries in her proclamation of the gospel, begun with the Gentile, often completely ignored the Jew, and during long periods of time never gotten to Jerusalem at all. This is a tragic and lamentable fact. It is a sin to be confessed and repented of. If the great apostle of the Gentiles had great heaviness and continual sorrow in his heart because of Israel, if the 'receiving' back of Israel will be 'life from the dead,' the conversion of the Jew should certainly figure very prominently in all plans and programs for world evangelization.

"This, we repeat, is the anomaly. If the promises to the Church are so glorious that the individual Jew does not lose anything, but greatly benefits by accepting them, why should not the reception of the nation of Israel into the Church be as great a blessing to the nation proportionally as to the individual? For if it is robbery to deprive the Jews as a nation of their nationalistic expectations, then it follows inevitably that the Jews who believe during the Church age and become members of the Church are in a sense being penalized and punished. Their admission into the Church is a kind of second-best. They are forever deprived of the kingdom blessings because their fathers rejected their Messiah and the time for the restoration of the kingdom is not yet; but as a matter of grace they are allowed membership in the Christian Church in which none of these earthly blessings are to be found. But, if the New Testament makes anything plain, it is that for the Jew as well as for the Gentile, for the Jew of the future quite as much as for the Jew of the present or the past, the greatest privilege and honor which can be his is to know Christ whom to know is everlasting life and to become a member of His glorious body, the Church of the living God."

This is all to the good. As to Dr. Allis' fallacies, we think we understand them. What he does not grasp, is the revelation that the Church will never convert the world in this age; that blindness *in part,* has happened unto Israel; and just as effectively has blindness *in part* happened to the Gentile world. Not *all* Jews will believe, nor will all Gentiles be converted. In fact, when we weigh in the balances, and consider for how many years the Gentiles have had the Gospel, and then look about us and see the world chaos and catastrophe rushing upon us as a tidal wave; when we see the so-called Church stripped of her power, divided within, ineffective without, dabbling in world politics where she has no business, making "religion" something to worship, instead of the Lord Jesus Christ, we wonder whether the Gentile world is not guilty of a greater treading under foot of the Precious Blood, than the Jews ever were? We wonder what *might have been* if only the Church had obeyed her God and had faithfully persisted in a Gospel program, "To the Jew First!" Pharaoh had it in his power to obey God and let Israel go. But he steeled himself against God. But that did not release Moses from going ten times to Pharaoh with his message. Is it not an inexcusable arrogance for any church to say, "We will *not* go to the Jews, they will not accept our message; but we *will* go only to the heathen"? We know of a church which boasts with self-righteous pride that it has over fifty missionaries in the foreign mission field. But ask them about the Jews, and they will look at you with blank amazement, and even mild disdain; not a dollar in a whole year to give the Jews the Gospel! Is this not truly and deplorably the shame of Christendom? Certainly, not all Jews will be saved; nor has the Church made any startling progress in saving all Gentiles. So, if you are cutting the Jews out of your missionary activities then, in all honesty, why don't you cut out the Gentiles? The astonishing truth is that where Jewish mission work is efficiently and ably carried on, the actual conversions are some 3½ to 1 as compared to Gentile results—money, population and effort being equal! Do you wonder that God told us to take the gospel "To the Jew First," and that the devil bitterly fights this policy, and blinds good, earnest Christian leaders to this staggering sin of omission?

A Rebuke Doubly Effective

But what an astonishing rebuke to the men who should have been militantly in the advance guard in giving the Gospel "To the Jew First!" Think what it means when a brother who makes no claim to any conviction from the Bible concerning the restoration of Israel to God's favor, and who seems to believe that in the Church is the complete consummation of all of God's redemptive program, writes a paragraph like this:

"The early Christians were instructed in their proclamation of the Gospel, to begin at Jerusalem. Both Peter and Paul began with the Jew. But the Christian Church has for centuries . . . often completely neglected the Jew, and during long periods of time never gotten to Jerusalem at all. This is a tragic and lamentable fact. It is a sin to be confessed and repented of."

How our hearts would glow within us if some of our premillennial leaders should humbly bow the knee and make this sort of confession!

Can This Be Jew-Hate In A New Dress?

You may imagine our feelings when, for instance, we receive a letter from a prominent pastor in one of these leading "fundamentalist" churches, telling us bluntly that because we teach the doctrine, "to the Jew first," he will not allow any of our missionaries to speak in his church! What he really means to say is that because he does not like the kind of necktie we wear, or the way in which we comb our hair, he is going to deprive all the Jews from receiving the Gospel! This, strangely enough, is the very thing that Satan delights to accomplish. For if we are in the end-times it does not take much understanding of the Bible to know that the most important task before the Church is the intensive and speedy evangelization of the Jew. If Satan can side-track that, he can chortle in sardonic glee, for he has successfully cut at the very root of God's program for the end-time. What a sad comment it is that instead of these brethren thanking God that He has raised up for these end-time days such a tower of Gospel strength as this Jewish Mission has proved to be, and that He has kept us faithful and plodding day after day for these more than fifty years, until the Mission has come to be the largest, the most respected, the most beloved, and, yes, the most hated, Jewish mission agency in all the world,—that instead of praising God for this, instead of putting the shoulder to the wheel and saying joyfully, "Count us as among your faithful friends," instead of coming to the help of the Lord, these brethren actually tell us, "We have no use for you because you are teaching, 'To the Jew first.'" We wonder what God in His heaven must think of this when He looks down and sees such silly foibles and trivialities among those who profess to believe on His Name! When a horse has slipped on the icy pavement and lies on the ground in great suffering, the man who has the slightest quality of humaneness, does not stop to argue with the horse as to why he fell down, or to blame the horse for not having been more surefooted; no, the first thing any man of decency will do is to cry, "Up with the horse!"

Willful Evasion?

Ironically enough, these rebellious brethren have no Scripture to support their disobedience. All they offer is their personal *ipse dixit*, which means, in the last analysis, that they are pitting their "opinion" and their will against God. Still stands, majestic and undisputed, the divine declaration, "To the Jew First," of Romans 1:16. It has never been repealed, never canceled. Our challenge has been thrown out many times, i.e., produce one sentence in the Book in which this basic obligation is canceled! When the objectors propose that the text is *historic* only, that the Gospel *was* preached to the Jews, and that it no more applies, we answer immediately, "If it is historical, at least be consistent; for the verse also contains the phrase, 'And also to the Greek (Gentile),' and therefore that too is *historical;* so why don't you stop giving the Gospel to the Gentiles?" Then they lose their temper and hate the Jews all the more! The churches are becoming more and more paganized, and apostasy creeps over the organized system of Christendom, like a slow paralysis, until that sad day shall come when He shall have to fulfill the warning of the ages, "I will spue thee out of my mouth!" We wonder if this sin of depriving Israel of Gospel ministry, and the refusal to make Jewish missions an integral part of the program of the Church, will not be the actual final cause of the apostasy and the "spueing out?" For nowhere is the honor of God more deeply touched, or more acutely sensitive, than when it comes to how the Church and the world treat His people, Israel, "still beloved for the fathers' sakes." You see, we need desperately a conviction burned into our very souls in this matter, so that we will find ourselves crying out with Paul of old, "Woe is to me if I preach not the Gospel!" In this case, of course, we mean the Gospel to the Jews.

"Up With The Horse!"

Dear brother and dear sister, the people of Israel are in the most baffling straits in all their long sad history; they are prostrate, and in the throes of death agony. We say to you, we beg of you, we plead with you, in the name of all that is good and true and holy, please do not argue with us because you do not agree with our clear-cut standing by the Word of God in the matter of giving the Gospel to the Jew first, do not speculate as to what kind of future the Jew is going to have after you and I are out of this world; do not dabble or have dealings with those who take fiendish delight in besmirching and vilifying these helpless derelicts of world hate: but in God's name, put your shoulder to the wheel, and with a one, two, three, unite in the shout, "Up with the horse!" So it will be that when we meet the Lord face to face in that last day of accounting, each of us will stand before Him unashamed, and hear His blessed words, "Well done, thou good and faithful servant!"

The times are chaotic; nothing is gained by hiding this frightening fact; we are nearer the crisis of all time than the Pollyanna dreamers would have us believe. Jew-hate will by and by sweep the country with the desolation of a black fever epidemic. We need to ask God upon bended knee that He will keep us true. We need now to rise in our might, we to whom God has given the sure Word of truth, the light that shineth in a dark place, we in whose hearts He has planted a love unquenchable for His people, Israel; we must rise in our might and give the no uncertain answer as to where we stand in the matter of giving the Gospel "To the Jew first." And so mightily must we fling back the challenge to these misguided leaders that our voices shall reach to the citadels of heaven, and bring back the answering echo, "Lovest thou me? Feed my sheep!"

This Is The Acid Test

We come once more to the first month of the new year, and once more we announce to the precious members of our family, "The treasury of the Lord's house is now open to receive the gifts of His people so that the work of giving the Gospel to the Jew first shall continue unabated and in greater intensity than ever before in the history of the world." The measure of the loyalty of the child of God to the Lord Jesus Christ is the measure of his interest in the Jewish mission testimony. This is the acid test of Christian profession, and it is a challenge that cannot be evaded. Shall we not therefore rally about the Mission and give to it the greatest outpouring of affection and prayer and treasure that ever it has had in any previous January in all of its history? That will be the finest answer to the carping critics and the Jew haters, and the scandal mongers, and the envious, and all others who refuse to bow humbly before the Lord and ask Him in all simplicity, "Lord, what wilt thou have me to do?"

We close as we have done more than once in the days gone by, with the invitation of Moses to Hobab, "We are journeying unto the place of which the Lord said, I will give it you: come thou with us and we will do thee good; for the Lord has spoken good concerning Israel." Numbers 10:29. The Lord bless you out of Zion. May He make every good thing abound unto you. Many of our friends have heartaches; for many we pray, and shall continue to pray. What this year holds in store, only He who is the Creator of time, knows. But always we know our trust is in Him, and He doeth all things well.

IS THERE A GENTILE CHURCH?

(*Addendum*)

A question often heard in Christian circles when the Jewish problem engages attention, is this: "Is there a Gentile Church? What is the difference between the 'Times of the Gentiles' and the 'Fulness of the Gentiles'? Has the Jew been set aside until the 'Gentile Church' is completed? What *is* the Church?"

It is our conviction that we are living in the closing days of the Church dispensation. Because of this, the devil, knowing "that he hath but a short time" (Rev. 12:12) is busy in a final desperate effort to deceive all whom he can. We are not surprised, therefore, to note the confusion among many Christian people as to the place which God has given the Jew in the present age of grace. It is asserted, for instance, by several otherwise able teachers that these are the times of the Gentiles; that the Jews are set aside for the present; and that God is calling out a people from among the Gentiles for His name. One teacher goes so far as to talk of the "Gentile Church," forgetting that there is no such expression as the "Gentile Church" in the whole Bible! It is amazing to see how, through the influence of Romish teaching, so many Christians have misinterpreted this important Bible doctrine. Rome taught that the Jews are cast off now, and in doing so she served the devil effectively, for she put an effective check to Jewish mission work. Anti-semitism is increasing at a bewildering and staggering rate. The child of God needs to be continually on guard against this subtle device of Satan. For it is at this point that the devil comes to grips with God; and we surely do not wish to be found on the devil's side. Even Bible teachers are not immune to this treacherous deception. Notice how in recent times certain Christian leaders have fallen into the trap of Jew-hate. One, for instance, has allowed the venom of Jew-hate to possess his heart and mind so completely that he published and circulated widely a tract in which he calmly represented Joseph of Egypt as a racketeer and a communist! Joseph, the one whom God loved, and blessed, the one who, more than any other beautiful character of the Bible, is the finest type we have of the Lord Jesus Christ, this Joseph a communist and a racketeer! What a warning to true Christians to shun and condemn unhesitatingly every least manifestation of Jew-hate!

This same brother teaches that the Jews are a hopelessly lost brood, that they cannot be converted into the Church of Christ! In other words, the Holy Spirit is powerless to bring a Jew to Christ!

Recently another exposition of the expression, "The fulness of the Gentiles," was brought to our attention, and in that treatise the writer repeats the untenable proposition that this phrase means the ingathering of the Gentiles into the Church of Christ. He says, "The great work the Holy Spirit has come to do during the present age, *the times of the Gentiles,* is to call out *that* people for His Name, the Church!" (Italics ours.) Without realizing it, the writer contradicts himself by confusing "times of the Gentiles," a phrase which he previously asserts as referring exclusively to world dominion in politics, with the Holy Spirit's work of calling out a people unto God's Name! Such inconsistency is inevitable if one starts out with a false premise. This writer sinks even deeper into the quagmire of his own fallacious thinking, when he says, in the same article, " 'To the Jew first' has been done away with."

The devil knows that the evangelization of the Jews is

closely connected with our Lord's return, and naturally it is his wish to put that off as long as possible.

Let us study this matter thoroughly, and while we do so earnestly seek the Lord's guidance.

Suppose we start with the question, "What is the Church?" After that has been answered, we can, step by step, reach an understanding of the other questions.

What is the Church?

The word "church" is the Greek word Ecclesia, a called-out assembly of believers in the Lord Jesus Christ. The Bible explicitly teaches that in the Church there is neither Jew nor Greek, but it is composed of individuals from among all nations—Englishmen, Americans, Chinese, Japanese, Jews —all sharing equally in the body of Christ. Thus we speak of a Chinese Christian, a Hindu Christian, a Jewish Christian, etc. The early disciples preached to both Jew and Gentile, thus ruling out the idea of a Church composed of Gentiles only. They followed still more closely the divine order, for they always preached "to the Jew first" in each town where they went, and then after having given their testimony to the Jew first, they turned to the Gentiles. This is the only Scriptural method of preaching that God has ever authorized. Every other method which leaves out God's order "to the Jew first" is in direct disobedience to His revealed will.

When Rome came into power she sought a way to vent her hatred upon the Jew, and misused the Scriptures in her effort to secure Bible authority for her wicked practices. Accordingly, there came to the Jews a flood of persecution that has continued to the present day; and while we have shaken from ourselves much of the Romish wickedness, we still retain a few vestiges of her evil work. To bolster herself up in this doctrine of Jewish rejection, Rome took such passages as Acts 15:14 and Romans 11:25 and twisted them to mean that the present is a Gentile age. Acts 15:14 reads: "Simeon hath declared how God at the first did visit the Gentiles, to take out of them a people for His name." Romans 11:25 reads: "For I would not, brethren, that ye should be ignorant of this mystery, lest ye should be wise in your own conceits; that blindness in part has happened to Israel, until the fulness of the Gentiles be come in." There is not a shred of authority in these words for the Romish heresy. Acts 15:14, rendered freely from the original reads: "God for the first time did visit the Gentiles to take out of them a people for His Name." It does not say that God "did visit the Gentiles exclusively." Acts 10:45 throws light on this matter, for it reads: "And they of the circumcision which believed (Jewish believers) were astonished ... because that on the Gentiles *also* was poured out the gift of the Holy Ghost." In Acts 15:14 the noteworthy point is not that the Gentiles were to be made exclusive believers in Christ but that for the first time in history Gentiles *also* were to become partakers with Jews in the gift of the Holy Ghost.

Partial Blindness

Now let us examine the passage in Romans 11:25, "Blindness in part is happened to Israel, until the fulness of the Gentiles be come in." It is strange how Bible students seem to skip the words "in part." This verse teaches that a part of the Jews are blinded, while another part, the remnant, receive the Gospel gladly. But the Bible teaches the very same thing about the Gentiles, namely, that only a small remnant will receive the Gospel, while the great majority will reject Christ.

Is it not true then that the Church is composed of a

remnant from among all nations? Why then continue teaching the false doctrine that the Jews are set aside during the present age?

We think we know how this vicious error crept in: Because Jerusalem was destroyed by Titus, the Romish church seized upon that as proof that the Jews were cast off, ignoring the fact that the Jewish *national* dispersion had no relation to the *individual* Jew's opportunity of salvation.

Nationalism vs. Individualism

Let us examine afresh the teaching of Romans 11:25, already quoted. The apostle has been discussing in the preceding verses two distinct lines of truth, which we must always be careful to distinguish, namely, national rejection and individual election. The Jew is being punished *nationally* by a temporary suspension of the Abrahamic Covenant, a covenant that had to do solely with Israel's possession of the land of Palestine, in peace and prosperity. Israel's sin of rejecting her Messiah resulted in her being deprived of her land. She was driven out and scattered over the face of the earth. This is *national* punishment for *national* sin. But then is revealed a new mystery—the Church. It is established by its Divine Founder, the Lord Jesus Christ, and is a called-out body composed of both Jew and Gentile. The rule henceforth is "Whosoever will." This we call *individual election.* God is not now dealing with nations as such, whether Jew or Gentile, but with individuals. Therefore, the fact that the Jews nationally are set aside, driven out of the land, does not, cannot, affect the right of the individual Jew to become a child of God through personal faith in the Lord Jesus Christ! He thus classifies under the clear teaching of Ephesians 2:14-18:

"For he is our peace, who hath made both one, and hath broken down the middle wall of partition between us; having abolished in his flesh the enmity, even the law of commandments contained in ordinances; for to make in himself of twain one new man, so making peace; and that he might reconcile both unto God in one body by the cross, having slain the enmity thereby; and came and preached peace to you which were afar off, and to them that were nigh. For through him we *both* have access by one Spirit unto the Father."

Gentile World Power Begins

Now we come to the 25th verse of Romans 11, and here the Apostle turns to the *national* aspects of the problem, both as to the Jews and the Gentiles. He steps aside for a moment from the individual phase of Church election, and deals with God's national program. Blindness *in part* is happened to Israel nationally. Why? So that by Israel's *national* rejecting of the Lord Jesus Christ, God could judicially set them aside, and allow the full measure of Gentile iniquity to come to its climacteric head, as will be evidenced by the final crash of the Anti-Christ in the great Armageddon war, when Gentile power will be crushed by that "Stone cut without hands." This reign and testing of Gentile dominion began with Herod, the heathen, and will end with that last Herod, the Anti-Christ, who will blaspheme and defame God's Holy place.

The next verse, "And so all Israel shall be saved," now serves to clinch and rivet indestructibly the exposition just given. For it proves unimpeachably that *national* equations are involved:

"And so all Israel shall be saved: as it is written, There shall come out of Sion the Deliverer, and shall turn away ungodliness from Jacob: For this is my covenant unto them, when I shall take away their sins." Rom. 11:26, 27.

The word "saved" here means no longer the idea of salvation through the Grace of God in the Church—it is too late for that, for the Church will already have been caught up to be with the Lord when this phase of history appears—but "delivered," or "rescued." The reference is to such a verse as Zechariah 14:4, "His feet shall stand upon the Mount of Olives," to redeem the Jewish nation from the threatening destruction at the hands of the armies of the Anti-Christ. And that this is the plain and sure meaning of these verses, is further attested when we read, "For this is my covenant unto them when I shall take away their sins." That is, God now goes back to His Covenant relation with Israel, which means a restored *national* relation, a regathering to their own land, a re-establishing of the Throne of David.

The Fulness of the Gentiles

Perhaps we can reach a still better understanding by going back to God's covenant with Abraham. God's purpose in calling out Abraham and his seed was that through Israel he would be glorified among all nations. In other words, the Jews were called out by God to be missionaries among the Gentiles. The penalty for failing to do this was temporary expulsion from the land—the giving over of the land into Gentile hands until such time as the Jews would return again to God.

Sad to say, the Jewish nation became a failure in God's sight; they refused to go out among the Gentiles. So bad had they become that our Lord was compelled to denounce them in scathing terms. For this they rejected Him. What was the result? The nation was driven out of the land and God gave over the temporary jurisdiction of the land and the Jews to Gentile hands unto this day. This is what is meant by the expression, "the times of the Gentiles." From that time on the Jews were to be deprived of Palestine; the

Abrahamic covenant, dealing with the possession of the land, was put aside "until the fulness of the Gentiles be come in," that is, until the day of the Gentiles' testing shall be finished. If you will read carefully Romans 11:11, you will see that the reason why God brought salvation unto the Gentiles was that through the Gentiles He might win the Jew back to Him by causing the Gentiles to provoke them, the Jews, to jealousy. In other words, God called out Gentiles to become members of the Church, His body, in order that these Gentiles shall preach to the Jews, bring Jews back to Christ, and in this way make possible the early return of Christ to this earth as conditionally promised in Matt. 23:39, that whenever the Jews will believe in Christ He will come.

Gentile Monopoly

But what has happened? These Gentiles whom God called out to be partakers with the Jews in the spiritual blessings of the Church have become not partakers, but monopolizers, and have persuaded themselves that only to the Gentiles shall the Gospel be preached! This presents to us a second phase of Gentile failure; not only have the Christ-rejecting world powers abused the Jews and blasphemed God in the treading down of His Holy City of Jerusalem, but the Gentiles who have been professed followers of the Lord Jesus Christ have also failed, having neglected God's command to preach to the Jews. Soon, therefore, will be fulfilled the prophecy of Revelation 3:16, "I will spue thee out of my mouth." Why was the Jew driven out of Palestine? Because he refused to testify to the Gentiles. Why will God spue false Christendom out of His mouth? Because they refused to testify to the Jews.

Fulness of Gentile Iniquity

In other words, the "fulness of the Gentiles" simply

means that when the measure of Gentile iniquity and opportunity is full, God will again turn to the Jewish nation and carry out through them His program for the world's destiny. For illustration, read a passage like Genesis 15:16, "For the iniquity of the Amorites is not yet full." That is, God gave the Amorites a full opportunity, so that when He passed judgment upon them their iniquity was "full." Another passage will throw light on this interpretation, Daniel 8:23, "And in the latter time of their kingdom, when the transgressors are come to the full, a king of fierce countenance . . . shall stand up." Again we have the expression "full," meaning the full measure of sins.

What does it mean? It means that there is being written by the Gentiles themselves across the pages of their history the laconic word "full." Why is the world clutching at its own throat at this present moment with the whole world engaged in bloody war? Because the "fulness" of the Gentiles is about to come in. The Gentiles have failed.

A Gentile Church Unscriptural

What then is meant by the "fulness of the Gentiles"? Sometimes a fallacy can be exposed by the test of *reductio ad adsurdum*. Let us apply this method to the proposition that the "fulness of the Gentiles" means the completion of the Gentiles into the Church of Christ, and see how it works out:

First. Such a teaching contradicts every other passage of Scripture on this point. It would mean no Jewish missions, no Jewish conversions, but only an exclusive crusade among the Gentiles. Is there a Christian who would dare maintain such a wild theory as this? How strange that the clear statement, "blindness *in part*," which appears in the very verse under survey, is ignored! Can this be deliberate? Can it be possible that a Bible teacher who claims that "to the Jew first" has been done away with, is allowing his personal wish to be the father of his theology? Is there not need for a fresh self-examination here?

Second. Such a theory dishonors the character of God. Because a mob of Jews, egged on by the political henchmen of the hour, shouted "Crucify Him!" do you think God is going to condemn uncounted and unborn millions of Jews to an irrevocable hell without giving each individual Jew the same chance as each Gentile to become a child of God? No, God is not that kind of a God!

Third. It invalidates and nullifies all Jewish conversions, from the first disciple in Jerusalem, to the very latest Jewish convert of this twentieth century! No Peter, no Paul, no 3,000 at Pentecost! No Church! Nothing but hopeless fraud and chicanery! We might as well throw our Bibles away, for we are then become of all creatures most miserable! These erring interpreters forget that it is only because there was a Jew, Paul, that they now have the least hope for their own salvation!

Fourth. There would then be no Jewish remnant, as so clearly declared in Romans 11:5:

"Even so then at this present time also there is a remnant according to the election of grace."

"At this present time," refers of course to the present Church age. The solemn truth here is, that the Church can never be complete in His sight until that certain number of Jews, the *Remnant,* are brought into that Body, for which our Lord gave His blood, that the twain may be one! Are we deliberately, then, retarding His return for His Church because we are not helping Him to gather in this essential remnant?

The Meaning of Pleroma

It has been suggested that the Pleroma, translated Fulness, is used in Scripture only in connection with blessing and not with judgment. But a careful investigation will easily prove the error of this assumption. In addition to the references already mentioned under the heading "Fulness of Gentile Iniquity," we may cite one more example; in Galatians 4:4, we read, "But when the *Pleroma* (fulness) of the time was come, God sent forth his Son." Certainly there was no fulness of blessing either in Israel's historic development at that time, or in the status of the Gentile world. On the contrary, the whole world was in a state of corruption. As for Israel, that nation had about reached its lowest ebb of spiritual and material decline. So evidently, Pleroma does not mean "fulness of blessing" in this case. The honest thing to do is take it always in its own setting. If it means blessing, it will say so.

We are driven, therefore, to the inescapable truth that the expressions, "Fulness of the Gentiles" and "Times of the Gentiles," are identical and synonymous—there is no evading this important fact. Only once in all Scripture does there appear the phrase, "Times of the Gentiles." It is in Luke 21:24. Since the expression "Times of the Gentiles" has priority by about 30 years in Scripture usage, and since it is clearly defined by the Lord as having to do with Gentile world dominion, is it not logical and consistent, when we find the almost identical expressions in Romans 11:25, some 30 years later, to realize that it means exactly the same thing as the first use? Especially so, when the setting is the same, Gentile dominion and Jewish national restoration being directly contrasted? And more especially so, when there does not appear in Rom. 11:25 the slightest hint of any other meaning. Scripture is always its own best interpreter, and here we need no more powerful searchlight on Romans 11:25 than what we find in Luke 21:24.

To the Jew First—Today!

Moreover, those who arrogantly assert, " 'To the Jew first' has been done away with," are trifling with serious matters. Typically enough, they invariably fail to back it up with Scripture! It is purely an *ipse dixit*. But those who are better taught, have learned to challenge such an assertion by the question, "Where is it written?" And of course to such a question there is no answer. Even when they quote, "For there is no respect of persons with God," they have unwittingly and naively betrayed themselves; because this is the very passage which is their undoing, if only they will quote it in full! Here it is:

"Tribulation and anguish, upon every soul of man that doeth evil, of the Jew first, and also of the Gentile; but glory, honour, and peace, to every man that worketh good, to the Jew first, and also to the Gentile; for there is no respect of persons with God." Rom. 2:9-11.

When, in the apostolic days, the startling truth broke in with a blaze of light upon those early Jewish believers, that the Gospel plan of Salvation was intended for Gentiles as well as for Jews, the record tells us,

"When they heard these things, they held their peace, and glorified God, saying, Then hath God also to the Gentiles granted repentance unto life." Acts 11:18.

And Peter, Jew of Jews, brought face to face with the fact that Cornelius, a Gentile, had found salvation through a Jewish Christ, and through the ministry of a Jewish Peter, cries out with joy:

"Of a truth I perceive that God is no respecter of persons." Acts 10:34.

In other words, the early Jews rejoiced when they saw Gentiles come to the brightness of Israel's Messiah. "To the Gentiles also" had come salvation! And they glorified God! Is it not a blessed thing that now in the present age, God is raising up many of His children from among Gentile believers who are earnestly trying to "return the compliment"? They too, rejoice, and glorify God, when they hear of even one child of Abraham who has come into the fold of those "other sheep," so that there may be one fold and one Shepherd. And many of these faithful friends travail with us, in prayer, often with tears, in gifts, in living deeds of sacrifice, to the end that the last lost sheep of the House of Israel may be gathered into the Church, that it may be complete, and that the glad shout from heaven may come, when we shall be caught up to meet Him in the air, and so be forever with the Lord.

All Israel Shall Be Saved

There remains now the need of a word to explain "All Israel shall be saved (delivered)." By no stretch of the imagination can this be made to mean that every Jew, because he is a Jew, will be saved ultimately. There is no shred of Scripture to warrant such an optimistic assertion. There is no magic charm hanging over the Jew. It is eternally true that "There is none other name under heaven given among men, whereby we must be saved." Acts 4:12. This includes Jew as well as Gentile. A Jew who dies in the present age without Christ, is just as lost as a Gentile who passes on to the next world unsaved—God is no respecter of persons. All have sinned, and all need Christ. What a responsibility this lays on the heart of every child of God!

But the reference is to that black hour of history to come, sometimes known as the Great Tribulation, sometimes, as the Armageddon battle, and sometimes, and more correctly so, as "the time of Jacob's trouble." When that time comes, the Church will be no longer here, having been caught up to be with the Lord. Only the devil reigns supreme on the earth then. And Israel will undergo the greatest torment and agony of all her tragic history of suffering. God promises, "He (Jacob) shall be saved (delivered) out of it." Jer. 30:7. This is what Romans 11:26 has in prospect.

But, and this is even more tragic, God does not say *every* Jew living either now, or then, will be delivered. On the contrary, Zechariah reminds us that only one-third of the Jews then living, will be saved, or delivered! Zech. 13:8. So even if a Jew today should reject Christ, and, by some miraculous circumstance, should live to reach Jerusalem in the Day of Tribulation, he has no guarantee that he will be among the one-third that will survive to the hour of deliverance! Therefore, the burden of Jewish evangelization must lie all the heavier on the heart of the earnest child of God. The perilous position of the Jew becomes accentuated even more tragically than many have realized. Do you wonder that Jesus wept over Jerusalem? And should not the Church of Christ likewise weep, and labor, and pray in Israel's behalf?

Blessing Through Israel

Another consideration is often overlooked in this connection. Even the most rabid Hitlerite would admit that the Bible teaches no world blessings for the Gentiles *apart from Jewish blessing.* That is why Nazidom turned with such demoniacal fury on the Bible, and ordered it burned even in the churches. But the basic truth of Scripture teaching can be summed up in the verse of Ps. 67:7, "God shall bless us; and all the ends of the earth shall fear him." That is, it is only as Israel is blessed and is become reconciled to God, that the Gentile world can receive universal blessing. Only through a restored Israel can there be a restored world. And so the same principle applies in the Church itself, only of course in different degree. God is not now pouring out blessings on Gentile nations as such. On the contrary, He is testing them. Neither is God pouring out blessing on the Jewish nation—He is punishing Israel, as a nation. What then is He doing? He is gathering out a people, made up of individuals, for His Name! This people is from Jew *and* Gentile, not from Gentiles alone. And when they are thus gathered in, they become neither Jew, nor Gentile, but new creatures in Christ.

Life From the Dead

Now it is only reasonable to expect that just as *national* Israel, when restored to God, will bring blessings to the entire Gentile world, so when individual Jews are brought into the Church, blessings will redound to those who bring them in. That is, we have a right to expect that individual Jewish conversions now must bring individual blessings to the Gentiles in the Church. With convincing recurrence, this is exactly what has happened throughout the history of the Church, and is still happening. This also is what Scripture teaches; for Paul tells us, in speaking of the possibilities of Jewish conversion, in Rom. 11:15, "What shall their receiving (conversion) be, but life from the dead?"

The Jew in Church History

Abundant proof of the argument here presented is to be found in even a superficial glance over the pages of Church history. If we should take the first century of the Christian Era as our principal exhibit, we fear our opponents would be completely inundated by the veritable tidal wave of Jewish leadership and activity. But we will, out of kindly consideration for these "Gentile Church" enthusiasts, spare them the discomfiture. Instead, we will content ourselves with only a leaf out of the Church annals of the nineteenth century. And it must be a very small leaf at that, because our space is limited; for if one were to do justice to such a subject as the world influence of Christian Jews in the nineteenth century, he would require the volumes of a good sized encyclopedia. It must also be kept in mind that the nineteenth century was notorious for its exhibitions of Jew hate in all parts of the earth. Persecutions, banishments, robberies, drownings, burnings by fire, wholesale massacres—these are the murals that decorate the walls as we wander through the corridors of history. Yet even in the face of such a heart-breaking panorama, the heavens of nineteenth century Christianity are ablaze with the resplendent galaxies of Jewish stars—stars whose lights still shed their rays of illumination into our twentieth century of darkening gloom. We forget too easily the heroism of a Bishop Samuel Schereshewsky, to whom the heathen world will forever be indebted for his Mandarin Bible, a monumental work which enabled the Church to reach at one stroke 250,000,000 Chinese with the printed Word. And who will ever be able to appraise the value to the Church of an Alfred Edersheim? His "Life and Times of Jesus the Messiah," still towers above all other writings on the life of Christ. Or what shall we say of an Adolph Saphir, whose "Lectures on the Epistle to the Hebrews" have brought incalculable light and blessing to myriads of Bible students? Or of August Neander, the church historian?

Are all these out of place? Or are they not rather the semaphores of God, signalling to us, "This is the way, walk ye in it"?

Church for Jew and Gentile

So once more the Scriptures are proven to be wholly against the idea that this Church age is primarily or predominantly an age for Gentile blessing, except in so far as Gentiles by virtue of their preponderant population as compared to the Jews, can be said to predominate. It has been this erroneous assumption in the centuries gone by that has robbed the Church of her privileges with regard to the Jews.

That is why the Holy Spirit emphasizes, "to the Jew first." As to *preference*, there is none. As to method of approach, it is still *to the Jew first*. This order, or program, of Missions, has never been cancelled by God. He is indeed a bold adventurer in Scriptural exegesis who takes it upon himself to assert otherwise.

Let us love Israel; the Jew may have many characteristics that are unlovable; but God says, "I have loved thee with an everlasting love." So we will love because God loves. And perhaps sooner than we think that last Jew will be gathered in to complete His Church, which He loved even unto death; and then we who are His, shall be transported into His eternal presence; and how sweet will be the word of His approval to our ears, "Inasmuch as ye have done it unto the least of these my brethren, ye have done it unto Me!"